Selected Poems of May Sarton

Books by May Sarton

POETRY

Encounter in April
Inner Landscape
The Lion and the Rose
The Leaves of the Tree
The Land of Silence
In Time Like Air
Cloud, Stone, Sun, Vine
A Private Mythology
As Does New Hampshire
A Grain of Mustard Seed
A Durable Fire
Collected Poems (1930–1973)
Selected Poems

NOVELS

The Single Hound
The Bridge of Years
Shadow of a Man
A Shower of Summer Days
Faithful Are the Wounds
The Birth of a Grandfather
The Fur Person
The Small Room
Joanna and Ulysses
Mrs. Stevens Hears the Mermaids Singing
Miss Pickthorn and Mr. Hare
The Poet and the Donkey
Kinds of Love
As We Are Now
Crucial Conversations

NONFICTION

I Knew a Phoenix
Plant Dreaming Deep
Journal of a Solitude
A World of Light
The House by the Sea

Selected Poems of May Sarton

Edited and with an Introduction by
Serena Sue Hilsinger and Lois Brynes

W · W · NORTON & COMPANY
New York · London

W. W. Norton & Company, Inc., 500 Fifth Avenue, New York, N.Y. 10110
W. W. Norton & Company Ltd., 25 New Street Square, London EC4A 3NT

Published simultaneously in Canada by George J. McLeod Limited,
Toronto. Printed in the United States of America.

Library of Congress Cataloging in Publication Data

Sarton, May, 1912–
Selected poems of May Sarton.

Includes index.
I. Title.
PS3537.A832A17 1978 811'.5'2 78-14850
ISBN 0-393-04505-6
ISBN 0-393-04512-9 pbk.

4 5 6 7 8 9 0

Contents

Introduction

May Sarton is a contemporary writer of remarkable versatility and scope. The author of thirty-one volumes, she is at home in three genres—autobiography, fiction, and poetry—and she continues to work in all three. Her most recent book of memoirs, *The House by the Sea,* was published in 1977; her latest novel, *A Reckoning,* will be published in 1978; and she is currently preparing a new volume of poetry.

Although she is an indefatigable and compelling writer of journals and memoirs, it is in her poetry that May Sarton most reveals herself as a human being and an artist. The poems, written over a period of forty years, do not express an easy and comfortable movement toward arrival, resolution, and conclusion. Rather, they suggest an energetic alternation of mood, antithesis of idea, ebb and flow of experience. For the most part, these are poems of process rather than statement. Therefore, the arrangement of this selection is not chronological; instead, it attempts to preserve and to clarify the central rhythms of the poet's voice and vision.

May Sarton is neither the victim nor the champion of any particular subject matter, current of taste, literary technique, or tradition. The private moment of erotic love and the public event of Kent State are equally occasions for her poetry, and the voice to which these occasions give rise ranges from the pastoral to the polemical.

In form, these poems range from the closed couplet to a clean, tough deliberately dissonant free verse; the experience always dictates the form. For example, in "The Furies" the form is extremely strict: a series of sestets made up of trimeter couplets. Here is the final stanza:

Wrap you in glamour cold,
Warm you with fairy gold,
Till you grow fond and lazy,
Witty, perverse, and crazy,
And drink their health in wind,
And call the Furies kind.

The Furies here are, of course, not the ancient avengers but their more ordinary, though equally eternal, counterparts: illusion, sloth, and banality. The strict but simple form works well to convey their dailiness; however, their dangerous deceptiveness is also conveyed by the slightly cacophonous, hypermetrical third and fourth lines and by the final rhyme, which is sight but not sound.

In "At Delphi" the form is a spare, short-lined free verse. This poem is not about what was heard but about what was not heard. The message of the oracle is silence, and the unadorned, prosaic last lines express powerfully just how loud silence can be:

Everyone stands here
And listens. Listens.
Everyone stands here alone.

I tell you the gods are still alive
And they are not consoling.

I have not spoken of this
For three years,
But my ears still boom.

According to tradition, the messages of the oracle in ancient times were always delivered in metered verse. Here, modern times, she does not speak at all, and the poet can only speak of her in unmetered verse. These last lines of the poem speak not only of the oracle's silence but also of the poet's silence, now after three years finally broken, colloquially, even awkwardly, but very effectively, as the result of the melding of form and meaning.

In "At Delphi" collective tradition catalyzes private mythology. Generally, in Sarton's poetry, "time past and time present," art and life are inseparable; their relationships are reciprocal and dynamic; and the poet is the medium of their interaction.

The theme of artistic composition—as both past fact and present act—pervades these poems. Often the art of the past comes alive, is transformed into a moment of living experience. For example, the face of a sixteenth-century woman painted by Holbein becomes in a moment of light the face of the twentieth-century author Elizabeth Bowen. The present act of soothing a loved one by composing a lullaby brings Rousseau's canvas world alive, and both poet and listener become "part of the painter's dream."

In other poems this process is, in a sense, reversed—the living moment is spatialized and presented as a work of art. The daily miracle—the strut of a goose, the shriek of a parrot, a woman playing a cello or cutting a loaf of bread—when caught and celebrated by the poet, is released from time and given the reverence of form and "pure perspective." From the composed and composing imagination comes the living composition.

Art, love, solitude, nature: these, the usual subjects of poetry, are not in the work of May Sarton separate themes representing unconnected states of mind. In these poems love is a difficult collision of inner landscapes that may lead to a momentary transcendence, a joining in a shared, created world. Love is the source of poetry, but the process of poetry requires solitude. Solitude is often painful; the return to self, a dark reentry; but solitude is never a vacuum, never just an absence. Ultimately, solitude is a return to a changed inner landscape with renewed richness and energy. Thus the experience of love, though it is not sustained, does sustain; it adds to and changes the inner landscape, making it fertile and creative.

The creative process, with its rhythmic alternation of love and solitude, is echoed, with more than simply metaphoric power, by the natural world; and, even more significantly, the momentum of the creative process is often impelled by connection with the natural world. Whether it takes place in India, Greece, or the back garden, the meeting of inner and outer landscape is yet another productive collision.

The rhythms of this process are mysterious. Gods reside beneath the most ordinary ground. These gods inspire; but they are neither easy nor consoling, because they demand to be served, and are served, with first intensity by the human poet in every moment of her being.

Serena Sue Hilsinger
Lois Brynes

I

The Composed Imagination

. . . observing, recording
with a painter's impersonal eye.

"An Exchange of Gifts"

. . . the composed imagination reaches
Up and down to find its own frontier.
All landscapes crystallize and focus here.

"Journey toward Poetry"

Lady with a Falcon

Flemish Tapestry, Fifteenth Century

Gentleness and starvation tame
The falcon to this lady's wrist,
Natural flight hooded from blame
By what ironic fate or twist?

For now the hunched bird's contained flight
Pounces upon her inward air,
To plunder that mysterious night
Of poems blooded as the hare.

Heavy becomes the lady's hand,
And heavy bends the gentle head
Over her hunched and brooding bird
Until it is she who seems hooded.

Lady, your falcon is a peril,
Is starved, is mastered, but not kind.
The bird who sits your hand so gentle,
The captured hunter hunts your mind.

Better to starve the senseless wind
Than wrist a falcon's stop and start:
The bolt of flight you thought to bend
Plummets into your inmost heart.

The Lady and the Unicorn

The Cluny Tapestries

I am the unicorn and bow my head
You are the lady woven into history
And here forever we are bound in mystery
Our wine, Imagination, and our bread,
And I the unicorn who bows his head.

You are all interwoven in my history
And you and I have been most strangely wed
I am the unicorn and bow my head
And lay my wildness down upon your knee
You are the lady woven into history.

And here forever we are sweetly wed
With flowers and rabbits in the tapestry
You are the lady woven into history
Imagination is our bridal bed:
We lie ghostly upon it, no word said.

Among the flowers of the tapestry
I am the unicorn and by your bed
Come gently, gently to bow down my head,
Lay at your side this love, this mystery,
And call you lady of my tapestry.

I am the unicorn and bow my head
To one so sweetly lost, so strangely wed:

You sit forever under a small formal treee
Where I forever search your eyes to be

Rewarded with this shining tragedy
And know your beauty was not cast for me,

Know we are woven all in mystery,
The wound imagined where no one has bled,

My wild love chastened to this history
Where I before your eyes, bow down my head.

Nativity

Piero della Francesca

O cruel cloudless space,
And pale bare ground where the poor infant lies!
Why do we feel restored
As in a sacramental place?
Here Mystery is artifice,
And here a vision of such peace is stored,
Healing flows from it through our eyes.

Comfort and joy are near,
Not as we know them in the usual ways,
Personal and expected,
But utterly distilled and spare
Like a cool breath upon the air.
Emotion, it would seem, has been rejected
For a clear geometric praise.

Even the angels' stance
Is architectural in form:
They tell no story.
We see on each grave countenance,
Withheld as in a formal dance,
The awful joy, the serene glory:
It is the inscape keeps us warm.

Poised as a monument,
Thought rests, and in these balanced spaces
Images meditate;
Whatever Piero meant,
The strange impersonal does not relent:
Here is love, naked, lying in great state
On the bare ground, as in all human faces.

Baroque Image

For Any Artist

He angled the bright shield
To catch the setting sun,
And dazzled the whole field,
Enemy, friend, as one.

Who had the nerve to borrow
That sheen in a dark hour,
The arrows of Apollo
And the god's blinding power?

They did not sense the wound
Behind that tilted shield—
For he could hardly stand
Who dazzled the whole field!

Portrait by Holbein

For E. B.

In a moment exaggeration,
the brilliant image
exploding in the mind,
will fade like fireworks,
leaving it dark.
But for this moment
your face is there,
landscape by lightning:
Your face is drawn in pencil,
startling the sense
with its perfected shape,
the tension of the outline,
the curious created purity—
used as a painter would, yourself,
interpreted and mastered—
the comment of the mind.

Dutch Interior

Pieter de Hooch (1629–1682)

I recognize the quiet and the charm,
This safe enclosed room where a woman sews
And life is tempered, orderly, and calm.

Through the Dutch door, half-open, sunlight streams
And throws a pale square down on the red tiles.
The cosy black dog suns himself and dreams.

Even the bed is sheltered, it encloses,
A cupboard to keep people safe from harm,
Where copper glows with the warm flush of roses.

The atmosphere is all domestic, human,
Chaos subdued by the sheer power of need.
This is a room where I have lived as woman,

Lived too what the Dutch painter does not tell—
The wild skies overhead, dissolving, breaking,
And how that broken light is never still,

And how the roar of waves is always near,
What bitter tumult, treacherous and cold,
Attacks the solemn charm year after year!

It must be felt as peace won and maintained
Against those terrible antagonists—
How many from this quiet room have drowned?

How many left to go, drunk on the wind,
And take their ships into heartbreaking seas;
How many whom no woman's peace could bind?

Bent to her sewing, she looks drenched in calm.
Raw grief is disciplined to the fine thread.
But in her heart this woman is the storm;

Alive, deep in herself, holds wind and rain,
Remaking chaos into an intimate order
Where sometimes light flows through a windowpane.

Japanese Prints

On the Way to
to Lake Chuzen-ji

We regretted the rain,
Until we saw the mists
Floating the mountains
On their dragon tails.

Three Variations
on a Theme

The lovely slanting rain
And, across the fields,
The hesitating flight
Of parasols.

*

Lines of slanting rain
And, across the fields,
Many small moons—
The paper umbrellas.

*

Moths? Or notes in music?
The parasols float
Above the fields
In the slanting rain.

The Leopards
at Nanzen-ji

In the chill dark
Of an early spring morning,
The very soles of our feet
Are warmed
By the running of the leopards
On the golden screens!

*

So swift, no paw touches ground—
And we are drawn back
To look at them once more,
As by the leaping of a flame.

At Katsura,
Imperial Villa

In round straw hats,
Squatting in the rain
To weed the imperial moss—
Three mushrooms.

In a Bus

An infant boy
Stares, solemn,
At my nose,
Then reaches out to touch it . . .
Elephant's trunk?

Nursery Rhyme

For Polly, Whose Eyes Are Tired

Shut your eyes then
And let us slip
Out of the city rain
Into a special ship,
Call her The Pilgrim,
Set sail and go
Over the world's rim
To where Rousseau
Discovered a jungle
Of indigo trees,
A marvelous tangle:
Precise oranges,
Tigers with dreaming eyes,

Larger and larger flowers,
Leaves of gigantic size—
Wander for hours
Under a crimson sun
In a pale milky sky
With a vermilion
Lizard near by,
And over it all
The strangeness that hovers
Like a green pall,
Envelopes and covers
In a warm still suspense
All of the landscape
Like a sixth sense—
Till there is no escape,
Till in the grasses
(Two people Rousseau
Saw through his glasses
And wanted to know)
You who have shut your eyes
And I who brought you here
Are to our great surprise
Part of the atmosphere,
Part of the painter's dream,
Of his most intent seeing
In a place where things seem
Instead of being,
No longer living, no longer mortal,
Fabulous ladies,
Unreal, immortal—
Shut then your open eyes
Let us go softly home,
Back to the sleeping ship
Over the emerald foam,
Over the edge and slip
Out of the Rousseau world
Into the world of men,
Sails all bound up and furled:
Open your eyes again.

These Pure Arches

A Painting by Chirico
"The Delights of the Poet"

Here space, time, peace are given a habitation,
Perspective of pillar and arch, shadow on light,
A luminous evening where it can never be night.
This is the pure splendor of imagination.

To hold eternally present and forever still
The always fugitive, to make the essence clear,
Compose time and the moment as shadow in a square,
As these pure arches have been composed by will.

As by a kind of absence, feat of supersession
We can evoke a face long lost, long lost in death,
Or those hidden now in the wilderness of oppression—
Know the immortal breath upon the mortal breath:

A leaping out of the body to think, the sense
Of absence that precedes the stern work of creation.
Now when the future depends on our imagination,
Remember these pure arches and their imminence.

Journey toward Poetry

First that beautiful mad exploration
Through a multiple legend of landscape
When all roads open and then close again
Behind a car that rushes toward escape,
The mind shot out across foreign borders
To visionary and abrupt disorders.
The hills unwind and wind up on a spool;
Rivers leap out of their beds and run;
The pink geranium standing on the wall
Rests there a second, still, and then breaks open
To show far off the huge blood-red cathedral
Looming like magic against a bright blue sky;
And marble graveyards fall into the sea.

After the mad beautiful racing is done,
To be still, to be silent, to stand by a window
Where time not motion changes light to shadow,
Is to be present at the birth of creation.
Now from the falling chaos of sensation
A single image possesses the whole soul:
The field of wheat, the telegraph pole.
From them the composed imagination reaches
Up and down to find its own frontier.
All landscapes crystallize and focus here—
And in the distance stand five copper beeches.

Italian Garden

Where waterfalls in shining folds
Trouble the classic pools,
And always formal green enfolds
And frames the moving grays and golds—
Who breathes on stone, who makes the rules?

The dazzling spray of fountains
And sunlight flashing these
Silver and gold suspensions
Broken by leaves—
Who plays with these subtle and gay dimensions?

The cold triumphant stairs
Gentled by lichen and old moss
Rise up from watery lairs
Where light and shadow cross—
Who is received at these grave receptions?

Who past the long wall saunters on
Down the cool sheltered paths alone,
And at last climbs the lichened stair
To stand, astonished, in a bright blue air?

It's Poetry that's taken by surprise
In the most rigid of geometries.

Behind What Little Mirror . . .

Behind what little mirror lies the country of your voice?
What rivers the heart has seen but never the open eyes?
What was your instrument, what rainy flute your choice,
What lucid language, lighter than our human cries
Did you once speak to call this voice your own?
No bird could hold such grief in its slight throat,
No human anguish sing like light enmeshed in rain,
Is it a spirit then, composed of immaterial note—
And if you are that spirit in a mirror's face
How can one reach you, unreflected, in a human place?

Franz, a Goose

It is contagious as a dance,
The morning exultation of the goose
Whose inappropriate name is Franz.
Daily he comes, majestic and snow white,
To put his private pond to use,
To stand alone within the rite
And make ovations to pure self-delight.

As one long waving sleeve, he dips
Soft neck, blue eyes, and orange beak
Deep into waters where the magic sleeps,
Now up, now down, in hieratic bliss,
Gives them the dark caress they seek,
Then lifts that giant arm, weapon and grace,
To shake a rain of diamonds to the grass.

Can one describe superb-as-these ablutions,
This royal pomp as a mere daily wash?
The liquid phrase, the lovely repetitions?
His squawks are murmurs now. He sings.
Then with one huge triumphant splash
Enters the pond and beats his wings:
"I am the goose of geese, the king of kings!"

Who could resist such pride or pull it down?
Yet who resist one tentative caress,
To touch the silken neck that wears a crown?
I dare the irresistible in play,
To meet a cold blue eye and blazing hiss;
His person rises up in terrible dismay,
And talks of the indignity all day.

Followed at just two paces by his queen
(Possessive murmurs lead her gently on),
He makes his progress like a paladin,
Explains, complains of the awesome caress,
And how pomp trembled yet achieved disdain,
Assures her that he gave a fatal hiss,
Assures himself what a great goose he is.

Lament for Toby, a French Poodle

The great Toby is dead,
Courteous and discreet,
He of the noble head,
Remote and tragic air,
He of the trim black feet—
He's gone. He is nowhere.

Yet famous in New Hampshire
As one who fought and killed—
Dog-bane and dog-despair—
That prey that all resign,
The terrible and quilled,
Heraldic porcupine.

He will become a legend,
Black coat and royal nature,
So wounded he was blind,
As on a painted shield
Some lost heroic creature
Who fought and would not yield.

If we were brave as he,
Who'd ask to be wise?
We shall remember Toby:
When human courage fails,
Be dogged in just cause
As he before the quills.

A Parrot

My parrot is emerald green,
His tail feathers, marine.
He bears an orange half-moon
Over his ivory beak.
He must be believed to be seen,
This bird from a Rousseau wood.
When the urge is on him to speak,
He becomes too true to be good.

He uses his beak like a hook
To lift himself up with or break
Open a sunflower seed,
And his eye, in a bold white ring,
Has a lapidary look.
What a most astonishing bird,
Whose voice when he chooses to sing
Must be believed to be heard.

That stuttered staccato scream
Must be believed not to seem
The shriek of a witch in the room.
But he murmurs some muffled words
(Like someone who talks through a dream)
When he sits in the window and sees
The to-and-fro wings of wild birds
In the leafless improbable trees.

Eine Kleine Snailmusik

The snail watchers are interested in snails from all angles. . . . At the moment they are investigating the snail's reaction to music. "We have played to them on the harp in the garden and in the country on the pipe," said Mr. Heaton, "and we have taken them into the house and played to them on the piano."

The London Star

What soothes the angry snail?
What's music to his horn?
For the "Sonata Appassionata,"
He shows scorn,
And Handel
Makes the frail snail
Quail,
While Prokofieff
Gets no laugh,
And Tchaikovsky, I fear,
No tear.
Piano, pipe, and harp,
Dulcet or shrill,
Flat or sharp,
Indoors or in the garden,
Are willy-nilly
Silly
To the reserved, slow,
Sensitive
Snail,
Who prefers to live
Glissandissimo,
Pianissimo.

Song

Now let us honor with violin and flute
A woman set so deeply in devotion
That three times blasted to the root
Still she grew green and poured strength out.

Still she stood fair, providing the cool shade,
Compassion, the thousand leaves of mercy,
The cherishing green hope. Still like a tree she stood,
Clear comfort in the town and all the neighborhood.

Pure as the tree is pure, young
As the tree forever young, magnanimous
And natural, sweetly serving: for her the song,
For her the flute sound and the violin be strung.
    For her all love, all praise,
    All honor, as for trees
    In the hot summer days.

The Clavichord

She keeps her clavichord
As others keep delight, too light
To breathe, the secret word
No lover ever heard
Where the pure spirit lives
And garlands weaves.

To make the pure notes sigh
(Not of a human grief, too brief)
A sigh of such fragility
Her fingers' sweet agility
Must hold the horizontal line
In the stern power of design.

The secret breathed within
And never spoken, woken
By music; the garlands in
Her hands no one has seen.
She wreathes the air with green
And weaves the stillness in.

Girl with 'Cello

There had been no such music here until
A girl came in from falling dark and snow
To bring into this house her glowing 'cello
As if some silent, magic animal.

She sat, head bent, her long hair all aspill
Over the breathing wood, and drew the bow.
There had been no such music here until
A girl came in from falling dark and snow.

And she drew out that sound so like a wail,
A rich dark suffering joy, as if to show
All that a wrist holds and that fingers know
When they caress a magic animal.
There had been no such music here until
A girl came in from falling dark and snow.

A Celebration for George Sarton

I never saw my father old;
I never saw my father cold.
His stride, staccato vital,
His talk struck from pure metal
Simple as gold, and all his learning
Only to light a passion's burning.
So, beaming like a lesser god,
He bounced upon the earth he trod,
And people marveled on the street
At this stout man's impetuous feet.

Loved donkeys, children, awkward ducks,
Loved to retell old simple jokes;
Lived in a world of innocence
Where loneliness could be intense;
Wrote letters until very late,
Found comfort in an orange cat—
Rufus and George exchanged no word,
But while George worked his Rufus purred,
And neighbors looked up at his light,
Warmed by the scholar working late.

I never saw my father passive;
He was electrically massive.
He never hurried, so he said,
And yet a fire burned in his head;
He worked as poets work, for love,
And gathered in a world alive,
While black and white above his door
Spoke Mystery, the avatar—
An Arabic inscription flowed
Like singing: "In the name of God."

And when he died, he died so swift
His death was like a final gift.
He went out when the tide was full,
Still undiminished, bountiful;
The scholar and the gentle soul,

The passion and the life were whole.
And now death's wake is only praise,
As when a neighbor writes and says:
"I did not know your father, but
His light was there. I miss the light."

Evening Walk in France

When twilight comes, before it gets too late,
We swing behind us the heavy iron gate,

And as it clangs shut, stand a moment there
To taste the world, the larger open air,

And walk among the grandeur of the vines,
Those long rows written in imperfect lines,

Low massive trunks that bear the delicate
Insignia of leaves where grapes are set;

And here the sky is a great roofless room
Where late bees and late people wander home,

And here we walk on slowly through the dusk
And watch the long waves of the dark that mask

Black cypresses far off, and gently take
The sumptuous clouds and roofs within their wake,

Until the solid nearer haystacks seem
Like shadows looming ghostly out of dream,

And the stone farm becomes an ancient lair,
Dissolving into dusk—and is not there.

A dog barks, and a single lamp is lit.
We are two silent shadows crossing it.

Under the lamp a woman stands at rest,
Cutting a loaf of bread across her breast.

Composition

Here is the pond, here sky, and the long grasses
That lean over the water, a slow ripple
Under the slightest wandering air that passes
To shift the scene, translating flat to stipple
On still blue water and troubling the green masses.

Three elements are spaced and subtly joined
To rest the restless mind and lift us where
Nothing in us is baffled or constrained,
Who wake and sleep as casual as they are,
And contain earth, and water, and the wind.

Take blue; take green; take the pale gold sand;
Take the slow changing shimmer of the air;
Take a huge sky above a steadfast land;
Take love, the tiger ocean in its lair,
And gentle it like grass under the wind.

These Images Remain

These images remain, these classic landscapes
That lie, immense and quiet, behind eyes
Enlarged by love to think only in shapes
That compass time and frame the changing skies,
Triumph of arch, of spire, triumph of trees,
The pure perspective, the poignant formal scene.
Pursued by time, still we were given these;
Even the flames of spring seemed frozen green,
Fountains suspended crystal on the air,
And every open square could make us glad.
Where we stood once, once free to stand and stare,
Imagination wanders like a god.
These images exist. They have not changed,
Though we are caught by time, by time estranged.

II

Love

This cup holds grief and balm in equal measure,
Light, darkness. Who drinks from it must change.

"The Contemplation of Wisdom"

The poem begins here.

"An Exchange of Gifts"

An Exchange of Gifts

1

"When you come
Every evening,
Carrying heavy trays,
Kneeling to serve us,
You of the lovely middle-aged face
And sad eyes,
And never raise your lids,
Your dignity humbles.
Who are you?
What is your name?"

Kyoko translated for me.
But would the hermetic person
Accept the gift?

"My name is Eiko," she said,
And vanished,
Leaving us abashed,
Lacking a smile.

A week later,
After her day off,
She brought me a long box,
And in it a delicate fan.
Gravely we each bowed low,
Having exchanged presents,
And then at last,
Like the moon
From behind a cloud,
We saw her radiance.

2

Now it is coming to an end,
I see how I have lived,
Observing, recording
With a painter's impersonal eye:
Plum blossom,

White butterflies
Against a dark pine.
That feathery elegance, bamboo.
That fabulous mountain, a small rock.

So it has been for three weeks,
Until a single tired face,
The face of a servant,
Broke the pane of glass
Between me and all things:
I am inside the landscape.

For the Japanese
The nape of a neck
May evoke passion.
A tired face
Grounded my lightning.

The poems begin here

Invocation

Come out of the dark earth
Here where the minerals
Glow in their stone cells
Deeper than seed or birth.

Come under the strong wave
Here where the tug goes
As the tide turns and flows
Below that architrave.

Come into the pure air
Above all heaviness
Of storm and cloud to this
Light-possessed atmosphere.

Come into, out of, under
The earth, the wave, the air.
Love, touch us everywhere
With primeval candor.

Prothalamion

How pure the hearts of lovers as they walk
Through the rich quiet fields
Where the stiff wheat grows heavy on the stalk,
And over barley and its paler golds
The air is bright—

Would touch it all, embrace, learn it by hand,
Plunging their faces into the thick grain,
To stroke as well as see the cow's soft flank,
To feel the beech trunk harsh under the palm,
And oh, to drink the light!

They do not even walk yet hand in hand,
But every sense is pricked alive so sharp
That life breathes through them from the burning land,
And they could use the wind itself for harp,
And pluck the vibrant green.

At first the whole world opens into sense:
They learn their love by looking at the wheat,
And there let fall all that was shy and tense
To walk the season slowly on propitious feet
And be all they have seen.

While all around them earth moves toward an end,
The gold turning to bronze, the barley tasseled,
Where the great sheaves will be stored up and bend
Their heads together in that rich wedding bed
All are about to enter.

The hearts of lovers as they walk, how pure;
How cool the wind upon the open palm
As they move on toward harvest, and so sure
Even this ripening has a marvelous calm
And a still center.

Death and the Lovers

For a time it is part of the machinery
Of feeling, one of the several counters
In the game: romantic love encounters
Death, and death is romantic scenery,
A stage device for deepening the view,
Papier-mâché of course. It can't be true.

Later it will become the central fact,
Not in imagination's realm at all,
But reckoned with, an implacable fall,
And to be felt under every wish or act—
The kiss, straight from the terrible heart
That will not beat forever, must, does hurt.

Death becomes real, and love is forced to grow.
These lovers do not turn away to weep,
But hold carefully all they have to keep,
And stare long at all they have to know.
When every gesture is made upon a quicksand,
Touch must be absolute and firm the hand.

Not by not seeing, but by seeing through:
With fresh clear eyes they search out each other,
As once the infant searched to find the mother,
And make a strong one out of a frail two.
These lovers, who have learned to reckon death,
Are gravely married on the moment's breath.

We Sat Smoking at a Table . . .

We sat smoking at a table by the river
And then suddenly in the silence someone said,
"Look at the sunlight on the apple tree there shiver:
I shall remember that long after I am dead."
Together we all turned to see how the tree shook,
How it sparkled and seemed spun out of green and gold,
And we thought that hour, that light and our long mutual look
Might warm us each someday when we were cold.

And I thought of your face that sweeps over me like light,
Like the sun on the apple making a lovely show,
So one seeing it marveled the other night,
Turned to me saying, "What is it in your heart? You glow."—
Not guessing that on my face he saw the singular
Reflection of your grace like fire on snow—
And loved you there.

Evening Music

We enter this evening as we enter a quartet
Listening again for its particular note
The interval where all seems possible,
Order within time when action is suspended
And we are pure in heart, perfect in will.
We enter the evening whole and well-defended
But at the quick of self, intense detachment
That is a point of burning far from passion—
And this, we know, is what we always meant
And even love must learn it in some fashion,
To move like formal music through the heart,
To be achieved like some high difficult art.

We enter the evening as we enter a quartet
Listening again for its particular note
Which is your note, perhaps, your special gift,
A detached joy that flowers and makes bloom
The longest silence in the silent room—
And there would be no music if you left.

A Light Left On

In the evening we came back
Into our yellow room,
For a moment taken aback
To find the light left on,
Falling on silent flowers,
Table, book, empty chair
While we had gone elsewhere,
Had been away for hours.

When we came home together
We found the inside weather.
All of our love unended
The quiet light demanded,
And we gave, in a look
At yellow walls and open book.
The deepest world we share
And do not talk about
But have to have, was there,
And by that light found out.

from *Autumn Sonnets*

If I can let you go as trees let go
Their leaves, so casually, one by one;
If I can come to know what they do know,
That fall is the release, the consummation,
Then fear of time and the uncertain fruit
Would not distemper the great lucid skies
This strangest autumn, mellow and acute.
If I can take the dark with open eyes
And call it seasonal, not harsh or strange
(For love itself may need a time of sleep),
And, treelike, stand unmoved before the change,
Lose what I lose to keep what I can keep,
The strong root still alive under the snow,
Love will endure—if I can let you go.

As if the house were dying or already dead;
As if nobody cared—and, in fact, who does?
(Whose feet but mine wear out the painted tread?
Who listens for the fly's autumnal buzz?
Who climbs the stair to a wide upstairs bed?);
As if the house were prepared every day
By an odd owner with madness in her head
For visitors who never come to stay,
For love that has no time here or elsewhere,
Who keeps fresh flowers on each mantel still,
And sweeps the hearth and warms the chilling air
As if to keep the house alive on will—
Truth is, her daily battle is with death,
Back to the wall and fighting for each breath.

For steadfast flame wood must be seasoned,
And if love can be trusted to last out,
Then it must first be disciplined and reasoned
To take all weathers, absences, and doubt.
No resinous pine for this, but the hard oak
Slow to catch fire, would see us through a year.
We learned to temper words before we spoke,
To force the furies back, learned to forbear,

In silence to wait out erratic storm,
And bury tumult when we were apart.
The fires were banked to keep a winter warm
With heart of oak instead of resinous heart,
And in this testing year beyond desire
Began to move toward durable fire.

The Snow Light

In the snow light,
In the swan light,
In the white-on-white light
Of a winter storm,
My delight and your delight
Kept each other warm.

The next afternoon—
And love gone so soon!—
I met myself alone
In a windless calm,
Silenced at the bone
After the white storm.

What more was to come?
Out from the cocoon,
In the silent room,
Pouring out white light,
Amaryllis bloom
Opened in the night.

The cool petals shone
Like some winter moon
Or shadow of a swan,
Echoing the light
After you were gone
Of our white-on-white.

Moth in the Schoolroom

Over night it had emerged
From the contorted bisque shell
Of its cocoon
In a small cage
In the schoolroom.

We watched it,
Fragile furred antennae,
Wings still damp and wrinkled
Feeling their way
Toward this new incarnation,
And their slow, slow
Pulsation.

I stood there beside you
After another meeting,
Close to another parting,
And thought of our mothlike love—
The cocoons of separation,
The cramped hard times,
And wings pulsing slowly
After we come together.

How long has love to live
So close to hope,
So close to caged?
Now it is death again
In the cocoon
That limits and contorts.
The exquisite moth
Its velvet softness,
Is a slow worm
Waiting and suffering
Toward huge quiet wings.

A Storm of Angels

Anarchic anger came to beat us down,
Until from all that battering we went numb
Like ravaged trees after a hurricane.
But in its wake we saw fierce angels come—
Not gentle and not kind—who threshed the grain
With their harsh wings, winnowed from waste.
They brought love to its knees in fearful pain.
Such angels come after the storm is past
As messengers of a true power denied.
They beat us down. For love, they thrash us free,
Down to the truth itself, stripped of our pride.
On those harsh winds they bring us agony.
Theirs is an act of grace, and it is given
To those in Hell who can imagine Heaven.

from *A Divorce of Lovers*

I shall not see the end of this unweaving.
I shall lie dead in any narrow ditch
Before they are unwoven, love and grieving,
And our lives separated stitch by stitch.
I shall be dead before this task is done,
Not for a moment give you your cool head.
Say we had twenty years and now have none—
Are you Old Fate itself to snap the thread,
And to cut both your life and mine in half
Before the whole design is written clear?
This tapestry will not unweave itself,
Nor I spend what is left of me to tear
Your bright thread out: let unfulfilled design
Stand as your tragic epitaph, and mine.

What price serenity these cruel days?
Your silence and ungiving, my small cries,
Followed by hours when I can lift some praise
And make the wound sing as in Paradise.
What price the poise you ask for, the unharried?
Four rooted years torn up without a qualm,
A past not dead perhaps, but quickly buried:
On one side anguish, on the other calm,
Both terrible because deprived of hope
Like living eyes still open in a grave.
And we shall lunch, you say, that is our scope.
Between what we have lost and still might save
Lies, very quiet, what was once too human,
And lovely, and beloved, a living woman.

Dear fellow-sufferer, dear cruelty,
"I feel so married to you," once you said,
And it is you who now unmarry me.
I wish I could hold fast your tired head,
Or bind up all the wounds that we have made,
Say that I never hurt, you never saddened,
Say we were good and peaceful, undismayed—
The truth is that we always wounded, maddened,
Tore every joy out of such pain, it is
No wonder that the battle nearly killed.

From such inhuman ways you wish to save us:
Oh, is it better now, all anguish stilled?
Tell me what sovereign remedy you found
To call this better, this one mortal wound?

Your greatness withers when it shuts out grief
And must assert itself through the denying
Of what was lately sap and the green leaf,
And this new stance resembles only dying.
Castrati have pure voices, as we know;
But the mature, who mutilate by choice,
Who cut the heart out so that they may grow,
What sweetness flows from such a tortured voice?
So you would gather in and cherish power,
"Today I have grown old," is your decree;
You cut down passion like a summer flower,
And chill the ripening season's warmth in me,
Whose strength was wiser when you could enfold
Another in your arms against the cold.

So drive back hating Love and loving Hate
To where, until we met, they had been thrown
Since infancy: forever lock that gate
And let them lacerate themselves alone,
Wild animals we never learned to tame,
But faced in growing anguish through the mist,
Elusive beasts we did not dare to name,
And whom we could not dominate or trust.
Now bury childish hunger, childish greed
In play-pen, zoo-pen, whatever pen will hold
The wild frustration and the starving need:
This is your method, so I have been told.
And mine? Stand fast, and face the animal
With the full force and pardon of the soul.

It does not mean that we shall find the place
Called peaceable in the old hopeful prints,
Where every tiger has a human face,
And every lamb can make a lion wince.
We met too late to know our meeting kind,

Too late for me to educate your heart,
Too late for you to educate my mind.
We shall be hurt again, and badly hurt;
There are torrents we cannot ever wall,
And there are arid deserts still to cross.
We shall not come where the green mercies fall,
To perfect grace, nor forget cruel loss—
But if we turn back now in such distress,
How find the way out of this wilderness?

For all the loving words and difficult
Work on the unregenerate heart, we foundered
Upon the seaming of a secret fault,
As rocks, mined by a flaw, are slowly sundered.
The need that joined us was too young and strong,
Yielding to violence and rage too soon,
Our every insight wrenched from some weak wrong.
This adult passion cried for a child's moon.
Not all the tenderness could set us free,
Nor all the steadfast hope through all the pain:
You never have been, you will never be
(The rock falls here, the secret flaw is plain)
My father, nor my son, nor any kin.
Where these words end, let solitude begin.

As I look out on the long swell of fields
Where winter wheat grows sparsely through the snow
And all lies fallow for those later yields,
Abandoned, quiet, where the pheasants go;
As skies move in slow motion overhead
To launch the wind and rain in a long gust,
Cold waves of air breaking on every homestead,
I beg my heart to lie still at long last.
But it thuds on, this animal gone blind,
And still enduring what strange marathon?
I must regard it with an acid mind:
Have done, poor beast, I say to it, have done,
And let pure thought rest on the winter sky
Without your stubborn question and reply.

Where do I go? Nowhere. And who am I
Who sit alone in this small silent ark?
No one and no thing, but a breath or sigh,
Receptacle of light and flooding dark.
Now sunlight ripples through me in long waves,
Now the night rises, a tremendous tide,
And I am drowned or nearly. That what saves?
Who is the bridegroom of this ghostly bride?
A thinking heart, a feeling mind stripped bare
Of warmth and flesh, the soft delight and thong,
Reduced to a fine bone, as thin and spare,
I may now make an instrument for song:
Poetry, pour through me your ruthless word
As strong as once was love that used me hard.

The Swans

I think this was a dream, and yet we saw
The stone bridge and the still canal,
And I remember how laburnum threw
A gold rain on the water very well—
After all, what we saw may have been true.

There in a rocky angle the two swans
On a small platform fashioned like a stage
In all that watery world were rooted ones,
And face to face, the snowy double image
Stood entranced there among the ancient stones.

Then as we watched the ritual play began;
They arched their wings full-span and shivered once,
Then gravely bowed their heads, and swan to swan
Lifted their heavy bodies in the dance,
Their long necks sinuous upon the silence,

Their long necks writing figures on the air
As if, like skates on ice, their beaks must draw
A precise pattern, and, what was written there,
Repeated with a concentrated awe,
Until the tension seemed too great to bear.

In one ecstatic motion, straight and pure,
The weaving necks were lifted, and each now
Stretched to the sky, as if it could endure
The little space between them better so,
And trembled! How immaculate they were!

Who would not pray, looking at such a scene,
To be alive, passionate, part of the dance,
And gladly yielding up all that is human
Become a part of natural delight for once,
Lovers take on the grave shape of the swan?

Der Abschied

Now frost has broken summer like a glass,
This house and I resume our conversations;
The floors whisper a message as I pass,
I wander up and down these empty rooms
That have become my intimate relations,
Brimmed with your presence where your absence blooms—
And did you come at last, come home, to tell
How all fulfillment tastes of a farewell?

Here is the room where you lay down full length
That whole first day, to read, and hardly stirred,
As if arrival had taken all your strength;
Here is the table where you bent to write
The morning through, and silence spoke its word;
And here beside the fire we talked, as night
Came slowly from the wood across the meadow
To frame half of our brilliant world in shadow.

The rich fulfillment came; we held it all;
Four years of struggle brought us to this season,
Then in one week our summer turned to fall;
The air chilled and we sensed the chill in us,
The passionate journey ending in sweet reason.
The autumn light was there, frost on the grass.
And did you come at last, come home, to tell
How all fulfillment tastes of a farewell?

Departure is the constant at this stage;
And all we know is that we cannot stop,
However much the childish heart may rage.
We are still outward-bound to obligations
And, radiant centers, life must drink us up,
Devour our strength in multiple relations.
Yet I still question in these empty rooms
Brimmed with your presence where your absence blooms,

What stays that can outlast these deprivations?
Now, peopled by the dead, and ourselves dying,

The house and I resume old conversations:
What stays? Perhaps some autumn tenderness,
A different strength that forbids youthful sighing.
Though frost has broken summer like a glass,
Know, as we hear the thudding apples fall,
Not ripeness but the suffering change is all.

In Time Like Air

Consider the mysterious salt:
In water it must disappear.
It has no self. It knows no fault.
Not even sight may apprehend it.
No one may gather it or spend it.
It is dissolved and everywhere.

But, out of water into air,
It must resolve into a presence,
Precise and tangible and here.
Faultlessly pure, faultlessly white,
It crystallizes in our sight
And has defined itself to essence.

What element dissolves the soul
So it may be both found and lost,
In what suspended as a whole?
What is the element so blest
That there identity can rest
As salt in the clear water cast?

Love, in its early transformation,
And only love, may so design it
That the self flows in pure sensation,
Is all dissolved, and found at last
Without a future or a past,
And a whole life suspended in it.

The faultless crystal of detachment
Comes after, cannot be created
Without the first intense attachment.
Even the saints achieve this slowly;
For us, more human and less holy,
In time like air is essence stated.

Strangers

There have been two strangers
Who met within a wood
And looked once at each other
Where they stood.

And there have been two strangers
Who met among the heather
And did not look at all
But lay down together.

And there have been two strangers
Who met one April day
And looked long at each other,
And went their way.

III

Solitude

Before we part, give me your love.
I'll use it as the key to solitude.

"The Contemplation of Wisdom"

I can tell you that solitude
Is not all exaltation, inner space
Where the soul breathes and work can be done.
Solitude exposes the nerve,
Raises up ghosts.
The past, never at rest, flows through it.

"Gestalt at Sixty"

Return

It is time I came back to my real life
After this voyage to an island with no name,
Where I lay down at sunrise drunk with light.

Here are books, paper, and my little knife,
The walls of solitude from which I came,
Here is the sobering, meditative night,

The quiet room where it is dark and cool.
After the intense green and the flame,
The flat white walls, the table are each good.

Long hours of work and the imposed rule:
That was the time of the tremendous rain,
The place of lightning, of the great flood.

This is the time when voyagers return
With a mad longing for known customs and things,
Where joy in an old pencil is not absurd.

What was fire is music. Then the heart was torn.
But tears are indulgence. Memory sings.
I speak of an island. Passion is the word.

Greeting

New Year's Eve, 1937

The earth feels old tonight
And we who live and stand on the cold rim
Face a new year.
It is raining everywhere
As if the rain were mercy,
As if the rain were peace,
Peace falling on our hair.
Open your hearts tonight; let them burn!
Let them light a way in the dark.
Let them one by one affirm
There is hope for a staff:
I say it will flower in our hands,
We shall go garlanded.
There is the fine fresh stuff of faith for a coat:
We shall go warm.
We shall go on by the light of our hearts.
We shall burn mightily in the new year.
We shall go on together—
O you who stand alone on the rim of the earth and are cold,
I salute you here!

Where Dream Begins

Strip off kindness,
Strip off shelter,
Stripped down, friendless,
Nor pride, nor warm shoes,
Nor any covering
A cold man might use
When there is no sun,
When heart is gone.

Without coat or cape,
Shoestring or doorlatch,
Or one cosy hope,
Stripped of odds and ends,
Even at last of love,
Where the world ends,
Go rich in poverty,
Go rich in poetry.

This nothingness
Is plenitude,
Honeycomb wilderness
Where the wild hare runs,
Wind in the torn seams,
Where rise buried suns,
Where darkness begins.
Here dream begins.

Christmas Letter to a Psychiatrist

1970

1

These bulbs forgotten in a cellar,
Pushing up through the dark their wan white shoots,
Trying to live—their hopeless hope
Has been with me like an illness
The image of what tries to be born
For twenty years or more,
But dies for lack of light.

Today I saw it again in the stare
Of the homeless cat, that hunger
Not for food only, but to be taken in,
And to trust enough to risk it . . .
Shelter, life itself. Can I tame her?
Come the worst cold, will she freeze?

How marvelous to know you can save,
Restore, nourish the abandoned,
That the life line is there
In your wise hands, Marynia!

2

"Yes," you say, "of course at Christmas
Half the world is suicidal."
And you are there. You answer the phone—
The wry voice with laughter in it.
Again and again the life line is thrown out.
There is no end to the work of salvage
In the drowning high seas of Christmas
When loneliness, in the name of Christ
(That longing!), attacks the world.

3

One by one, they come from their wilderness
Like shy wild animals
Weeping blood from their wounds,

Wounds they dare not look at
And cannot bind or heal alone.

What is it that happens then
In the small closed room
Where someone listens,
Where someone answers,
Where someone cares,
Whom they cannot hurt
With their sharp infant teeth,
With their sharp old antlers?

What does she do,
This doctor, this angel,
Who holds so many
In her human hands?
How does she heal the animal pain
So the soul may live?

4

No Ceres, she, no Aphrodite;
She cannot provide the harvest
Nor the longed-for love.

This angel must be anarchic,
Fierce, full of laughter,
Will neither punish
Nor give absolution,
Is always acute, sometimes harsh.
Still the impersonal wing
Does shelter, provides a place, a climate
Where the soul can meet itself at last.

There is no way out,
Only the way deeper and deeper inward.
There are no solutions,
But every word is action,
As is every silence.
On a good day the patient
Has used his reason
To cut through secret evasions,

Secret fears,
Has experienced himself
As a complex whole.

But angels do not operate
By any means we can define.
They come when they are needed.
(I can tell you of the resonance,
The beat of wings
Threshing out truth
Long after the hour is past.)
When they have gone
The light-riddled spirit
Is as alone as ever,
But able to fly its course again
Through the most hostile sky.

5

I know what it is like, Marynia.
Once I watched a jay flopping, helpless,
In the snow outside this window—
I brought it in, managed to pull out the quill
Shot through just under the eye.
I know what it is to have to be brutal
Toward the badly crippled
In order to set them free.
Then it was Easter and I saw the jay
Fly off whole into the resurrected air.

Now it is Christmas
When infant love, vulnerable beyond our knowing,
Is born again to save the world.

And for whatever crucifixions it will suffer.
Angel, be blessed for your wings.

All Souls

Did someone say that there would be an end,
An end, Oh, an end, to love and mourning?
Such voices speak when sleep and waking blend,
The cold bleak voices of the early morning
When all the birds are dumb in dark November—
Remember and forget, forget, remember.

After the false night, warm true voices, wake!
Voice of the dead that touches the cold living,
Through the pale sunlight once more gravely speak.
Tell me again, while the last leaves are falling:
"Dear child, what has been once so interwoven
Cannot be raveled, nor the gift ungiven."

Now the dead move through all of us still glowing,
Mother and child, lover and lover mated,
Are wound and bound together and enflowing.
What has been plaited cannot be unplaited—
Only the strands grow richer with each loss
And memory makes kings and queens of us.

Dark into light, light into darkness, spin.
When all the birds have flown to some real haven,
We who find shelter in the warmth within,
Listen, and feel new-cherished, new-forgiven,
As the lost human voices speak through us and blend
Our complex love, our mourning without end.

A Hard Death

We have seen how dignity can be torn
From the naked dying or the newly born
By a loud voice or an ungentle presence,
Harshness of haste or lack of reverence;
How the hospital nurse may casually unbind
The suffering body from the lucid mind.
The spirit enclosed in that fragile shell
Cannot defend itself, must endure all.
And not only the dying, helpless in a bed,
Ask for a little pillow for the head,
A sip of water, a cool hand to bless:
The living have their lonely agonies.
"Is there compassion?" a friend asked me.
"Does it exist in another country?"

The busy living have no time to see
The flowers, so silent and so alive,
That paling to lavender of the anemone,
That purpling of the rose no one can save,
Dying, but at each second so complete
A photograph would show no slightest change.
Only the human eye, imperfect but aware,
Knows that the flower arrested on the air
Is flying through space, doing a dance
Toward the swift fall of petals, all at once.

God's Grace, given freely, we do not deserve,
But we can choose at least to see its ghost
On every face. Oh, we can wish to serve
Each other gently as we live, though lost.
We cannot save, be saved, but we can stand
Before each presence with gentle heart and hand;
Here in this place, in this time without belief,
Keep the channels open to each other's grief;
Never accept a death or life as strange
To its essence, but at each second be aware
How God is moving always through each flower
From birth to death in a multiple gesture

Of abnegation; and when the petals fall
Say it is beautiful and good, say it is well.

I saw my mother die and now I know
The spirit cannot be defended. It must go
Naked even of love at the very end.
"Take the flowers away" (Oh, she had been their friend!),
And we who ached could do nothing more—
She was detached and distant as a star.

Let us be gentle to each other this brief time
For we shall die in exile far from home,
Where even the flowers can no longer save.
Only the living can be healed by love.

Burial

The old man who had dug the small pit
Opened the two boxes with a penknife
And let the ashes fall down into it,
The ashes of this husband and his wife,
My father and my mother gently laid
Into the earth and mingled there for good.

We watched the wind breathe up an ashen breath
And blow thin smoke along the grass—
And that was all: the bitterness of death
Lifted to air, laid in the earth. All was
Terribly silent where four people stood
Tall in the air, believing what they could.

Of Grief

You thought it heartless
When my father fell down
Dead in his splendid prime,
Strong as a green oak thrown,
That all I did was praise
Death for this kindness,
Sang with a voice unbroken
Of the dear scholar's days,
His passion of a lifetime—
And my loss never spoken.

Judge of another's grief?
Weigh out that grief in tears?
I did not weep my father,
The rich, the fulfilled years.
What slow death have you known?
When no hope or belief
Can help, no loving care?
We watch and weep alone.
My heart broke for my mother.
I buried grief with her.

It is the incomplete,
The unfulfilled, the torn
That haunts our nights and days
And keeps us hunger-born.
Grief spills from our eyes,
Unwelcome, indiscreet,
As if sprung from a fault
As rivers seam a rock
And break through under shock.
We are shaken by guilt.

There are some griefs so loud
They could bring down the sky,
And there are griefs so still
None knows how deep they lie,
Endured, never expended.
There are old griefs so proud

They never speak a word;
They never can be mended.
And these nourish the will
And keep it iron-hard.

My Father's Death

After the laboring birth, the clean stripped hull
Glides down the ways and is gently set free,
The landlocked, launched; the cramped made bountiful—
Oh, grave great moment when ships take the sea!
Alone now in my life, no longer child,
This hour and its flood of mystery,
Where death and love are wholly reconciled,
Launches the ship of all my history.
Accomplished now is the last struggling birth,
I have slipped out from the embracing shore
Nor look for comfort to maternal earth.
I shall not be a daughter any more,
But through this final parting, all stripped down,
Launched on the tide of love, go out full grown.

Myself to Me

"Set the table and sweep the floor—
Love will not come back to this door.

Plant your bulbs, sow summer flowers.
These be your joys, these your powers.

A cat for comfort, wood to burn,
And changing light as seasons turn.

Long hours alone and work to do—
These are your strength. These are for you."

So spoke myself. I listened well;
I thought that self had truth to tell.

But love came back after many a year,
Love all unasked knocked at the door,

Love all unasked broke down the door,
To bring me pain as it did before,

To bring me back lost poetry,
And all I'd meant alone to be.

What does myself now say to me?
"Open the door to Mystery.

Gather the grapes from any vine,
And make rich wine, and make rich wine.

Out of the passion comes the form,
And only passion keeps it warm.

Set the table, sweep the floor—
Forget the lies you told before."

Winter Carol

Black mood, away!
For all that's marred
And was ill-starred,
It's a new day.
Here comes the jay!

Dagger for beak,
And crest pure pride,
Bold and black-eyed,
His voice a shriek,
He shames the weak.

He takes the day,
The cruel ice,
As cats take mice
In pouncing play.
Black mood, away!

Be gone, sad woe!
For all that's marred
And was ill-starred,
The bright blue bravo
Flies in, flies low.

Because What I Want Most Is Permanence

Because what I want most is permanence,
The long unwinding and continuous flow
Of subterranean rivers out of sense,
That nourish arid landscapes with their blue—
Poetry, prayer, or call it what you choose
That frees the complicated act of will
And makes the whole world both intense and still—
I set my mind to artful work and craft,
I set my heart on friendship, hard and fast
Against the wild inflaming wink of chance
And all sensations opened in a glance.
Oh blue Atlantis where the sailors dream
Their girls under the waves and in the foam—
I move another course. I'll not look down.

Because what I most want is permanence,
What I do best is bury fire now,
To bank the blaze within, and out of sense,
Where hidden fires and rivers burn and flow,
Create a world that is still and intense.
I come to you with only the straight gaze.
These are not hours of fire but years of praise,
The glass full to the brim, completely full,
But held in balance so no drop can spill.

Gestalt at Sixty

1

For ten years I have been rooted in these hills,
The changing light on landlocked lakes,
For ten years have called a mountain, friend,
Have been nourished by plants, still waters,
Trees in their seasons,
Have fought in this quiet place
For my *self*.

I can tell you that first winter
I heard the trees groan.
I heard the fierce lament
As if they were on the rack under the wind.
I too have groaned here,
Wept the wild winter tears.
I can tell you that solitude
Is not all exaltation, inner space
Where the soul breathes and work can be done.
Solitude exposes the nerve,
Raises up ghosts.
The past, never at rest, flows through it.

Who wakes in a house alone
Wakes to moments of panic.
(Will the roof fall in?
Shall I die today?)
Who wakes in a house alone
Wakes to inertia sometimes,
To fits of weeping for no reason.
Solitude swells the inner space
Like a balloon.
We are wafted hither and thither
On the air currents.
How to land it?

I worked out anguish in a garden.
Without the flowers,
The shadow of trees on snow, their punctuation,
I might not have survived.

I came here to create a world
As strong, renewable, fertile,
As the world of nature all around me—
Learned to clear myself as I have cleared the pasture,
Learned to wait,
Learned that change is always in the making
(Inner and outer) if one can be patient,
Learned to trust myself.

2

The house is receptacle of a hundred currents.
Letters pour in,
Rumor of the human ocean, never at rest,
Never still. . . .
Sometimes it deafens and numbs me.

I did not come here for society
In these years
When every meeting is collision,
The impact huge,
The reverberations slow to die down.
Yet what I have done here
I have not done alone,
Inhabited by a rich past of lives,
Inhabited also by the great dead,
By music, poetry—
Yeats, Valéry stalk through this house.
No day passes without a visitation—
Rilke, Mozart.
I am always a lover here,
Seized and shaken by love.

Lovers and friends,
I come to you starved
For all you have to give,
Nourished by the food of solitude,
A good instrument for all you have to tell me,
For all I have to tell you.
We talk of first and last things,
Listen to music together,

Climb the long hill to the cemetery
In autumn,
Take another road in spring
Toward newborn lambs.

No one comes to this house
Who is not changed.
I meet no one here who does not change me.

3

How rich and long the hours become,
How brief the years,
In this house of gathering,
This life about to enter its seventh decade.

I live like a baby
Who bursts into laughter
At a sunbeam on the wall,
Or like a very old woman
Entranced by the prick of stars
Through the leaves.

And now, as the fruit gathers
All the riches of summer
Into its compact world,
I feel richer than ever before,
And breathe a larger air.

I am not ready to die,
But I am learning to trust death
As I have trusted life.
I am moving
Toward a new freedom
Born of detachment,
And a sweeter grace—
Learning to let go.

I am not ready to die,
But as I approach sixty
I turn my face toward the sea.
I shall go where tides replace time,
Where my world will open to a far horizon.

Over the floating, never-still flux and change.
I shall go with the changes,
I shall look far out over golden grasses
And blue waters. . . .

There are no farewells.

Praise God for His mercies,
For His austere demands,
For His light
And for His darkness.

On Being Given Time

Sometimes it seems to be the inmost land
All children still inhabit when alone.
They play the game of morning without end,
And only lunch can bring them, startled, home
Bearing in triumph a small speckled stone.

Yet even for them, too much dispersal scatters;
What complex form the simplest game may hold!
And all we know of time that really matters
We've learned from moving clouds and waters
Where we see form and motion lightly meld.

Not the clock's tick and its relentless bind
But the long ripple that opens out beyond
The duck as he swims down the tranquil pond,
Or when a wandering, falling leaf may find
And follow the formal downpath of the wind.

It is, perhaps, our most complex creation,
A lovely skill we spend a lifetime learning,
Something between the world of pure sensation
And the world of pure thought, a new relation,
As if we held in balance the globe turning.

Even a year's not long, yet moments are.
This moment, yours and mine, and always given,
When the leaf falls, the ripple opens far,
And we go where all animals and children are,
The world is open. Love can breathe again.

Annunciation

In this suspense of ours before the fall,
Before the end, before the true beginning,
No word, no feeling can be pure or whole.
Bear the loss first, then the infant winning;
Agony first, and then the long farewell.
So the child leaves the parent torn at birth.
No one is perfect here, no one is well:
It is a time of fear and immolation.
First the hard journey down again to death
Without a saving word or a free breath,
And then the terrible annunciation:
And we are here alone upon the earth.

The angel comes and he is always grave.
Joy is announced as if it were despair.
Mary herself could do nothing to save,
Nothing at all but to believe and bear,
Nothing but to foresee that in the ending
Would lie the true beginning and the birth,
And all be broken down before the mending.
For there can never be annunciation
Without the human heart's descent to Hell.
And no ascension without the fearful fall.
The angel's wings foretold renunciation,
And left her there alone upon the earth.

These Were Her Nightly Journeys

O joie—mon abîme parle. J'ai retourné vers la lumière ma dernière profondeur!

Nietzsche

These were her nightly journeys made alone,
The prisoner of seas which cannot drown,
Forced to descend the vertical
Plunges of dream.
Though all day long she knew no fear would come
And freely walked (who once in dreams had flown),
At night, she fell.
Burdens returned to magnetize the bone,
And in her helpless sleep she was hurled down.

Waters were heavy round her; she was bound
To heaviness of falling, falling with no end,
Imprisoned plunge
Sucked by dense air;
Or, worse, vertiginous oceans with no floor.
She fell and must keep falling, nearly drowned,
Yet cling to the lunge,
Gasp for more breath, for falling must extend:
She would be dead if once she touched the ground.

Yet once on the voyage through the night, she was
Given (but how? but why?) the means of choice:
She might choose to ascend
The falling dream,
By some angelic power without a name
Reverse the motion, plunge into upwardness,
Know height without an end,
Density melt to air, silence yield a voice—
Within her fall she felt the pull of Grace.

Through the descending motion a strong thrust
Strengthened her upward against the fluid wall—
So splitting-fierce a tension,
Psychic strain,
She turned weak, dizzy for downwardness again,
But was upheld, drawn upward, upward to free air,

Felt herself all ascension,
And floated through blue spaces over all,
Needing no walls, suspended on pure trust.

And when she came back to cool daylight, found
That she brought with her from that mystic sleep
The saving true event,
The image raised
In glass at a great height where angels blazed,
And there, at Chartres, as the sun made its round,
One crimson angel sent
A bolt down to her human world to keep,
A bolt that struck her knees back to the ground,

A bolt that raised her heart to blazing height
And made the vertical the very thrust of hope,
And found its path at last
(Slow work of Grace)
Into the texture of the nightmare place,
Shot through the falling dream, entered her night,
Lifted her past
The watery dark burdens, the descending slope
Until she was both grounded and in flight.

Jonah

I come back from the belly of the whale
Bruised from the struggle with a living wall,
Drowned in a breathing dark, a huge heartbeat
That jolted helpless hands and useless feet,

Yet know it was not death, that vital warm,
Nor did the monster wish me any harm;
Only the prisoning was hard to bear
And three-weeks' need to burst back into air . . .

Slowly the drowned self must be strangled free
And lifted whole out of that inmost sea,
To lie newborn under compassionate sky,
As fragile as a babe, with welling eye.

Do not be anxious, for now all is well,
The sojourn over in that fluid Hell,
My heart is nourished on no more than air,
Since every breath I draw is answered prayer.

Humpty Dumpty

Pain can make a whole winter bright,
Like fever, force us to live deep and hard,
Betrayal focus in a peculiar light
All we have ever dreamed or known or heard,
And from great shocks we do recover.
Like Wright's hotel we have been fashioned
To take earthquake and stand upright still.
Alive among the wreckage, we discover
Death or ruin is not less impassioned
Than we ourselves, and not less terrible,
Since we nicely absorb and can use them all.

It is the small shock, hardly noticed
At the time, the slight increase of gloom,
Daily attrition loosening the fist,
The empty mailbox in the afternoon,
The loss of memory, the gradual weakening
Of fiery will, defiant to exist,
That slowly undermines the solid walls,
Until the building that withstood an earthquake
Falls clumsily among the usual days.
Our last courage has been subtly shaken:
When the cat dies, we are overtaken.

The Caged Bird

He was there in my room,
A wild bird in a cage,
But I was a guest and not for me
To open the gate and set him free
However great my gloom
And unrepenting rage.

But not to see and not to hear
Was difficult to try:
The small red bird burst into song
And sang so sweetly all day long
I knew his presence near
And his inquiring eye—

So we exchanged some words;
And then I scattered seed
And put fresh water in his pan
And cleaned the litter from the pen,
Wondering about caged birds,
What more this one might need.

But oh, when night came then
I started up in fear
At the fierce wing-beat of despair
Hurled at the bars, hurting the air,
And the heart wild within
As if a hawk were near.

The room was sealed and dark,
And that war all within
Where on the small cramped stage
The bird fought with his cage
And then lay beaten down,
Almost extinguished spark.

And I went back to bed,
Trembling, who nothing could,
As if this scene had grown so huge
It ripped apart all subterfuge,
And naked now as God,
I wept hot tears like blood.

At Muzot

In this land, Rilke's country if you will,
Nothing is closed or intact.
The mountains open out an airy world and spill
Height as an ethos. We live in the vertical.
Angels, often invoked, become a fact.

And they have names, Cloud, Stone, Sun, Vine,
But the names are interchangeable.
All meld together in making the same flowing design;
We drink conjunction in the mingled wine.
The journey is infinite and it is immobile.

This is what he found after all the busy wanderings,
This childhood dream of a lonely tower
Set in a mountain-meadow world where the air sings
And the names are interchangeable of cloud and flower.
This is what he found: the grass full of springs.

A sacramental earth; reality both stalked
and made the vision clear.
And here the living waters sprang up where he walked.
It was the clouds and not himself who talked.
Was he the ghost who felt himself so near?

At Muzot he stood at last at the intersection
Of God and self (nothing is closed).
The voice he heard came from dissolving stone.
Even the mountains ascended and were gone,
And he himself stood naked and disclosed.

Song

No, I will never forget you and your great eyes,
O animal and power.

You will be stalking
The wood where I am walking.

You will lie asleep
In the places where I weep,

And you will wake and move
In the first hour of love,

And in the second hour
Love flee before your power.

No, I will never forget you and your great eyes
Angel and challenger.

You will be there
Dressed in your wild hair
Angel and animal
Wherever I may dwell,
Wherever I may sleep
You have the dreams to keep.

Walking in the still landscape by the rock and the bone,
You will be beside me when I am most alone.

On a Winter Night

On a winter night
I sat alone
In a cold room,
Feeling old, strange
At the year's change,
In fire light.

Last fire of youth,
All brilliance burning,
And my year turning—
One dazzling rush,
Like a wild wish
Or blaze of truth.

First fire of age,
And the soft snow
Of ash below—
For the clean wood
The end was good;
For me, an image.

For then I saw
That fires, not I,
Burn down and die;
That flare of gold
Turns old, turns cold.
Not I. I grow.

Nor old, nor young,
The burning sprite
Of my delight,
A salamander
In fires of wonder,
Gives tongue, gives tongue!

IV

Nature

In early spring, so much a fall of will,
We struggle through muds of unreason,
We dig deep into caring and contention;
The cold unwieldy earth resists the spade.
But we contend to bring a difficult birth
Out from the lack of talent, partial scope,
And every failure of imagination.

"Mud Season"

And so the morning's gone. Was this to waste it
In a long foolish flowery meditation?
Time slides away, and how are we to taste it?
Within the floating world all is sensation.
And yet I see eternity's long wink
In these elusive games . . .

"A Flower-Arranging Summer"

The Garden of Childhood

A rich profusion of familiar flowers,
All sunflecked, checquered, alive to the wind;
A gentle explosion of light in bosks and bowers,
So natural it seemed but half designed;
The arbor, an ardor of roses and clematis,
The borders, a passion of stained-glass blue and white
With spires of lupin and foxglove, lilies and iris,
All troubled and shining between shadow and light—

Chaotic splendor framed by a clipped lawn
Spread out under a cluster of apple trees
Where empty chairs and table stand forlorn,
Emblems of all our summers and all our teas.
Here Franz the goose, a cock, a guinea hen,
Two ducks, a Persian cat, all begged for a crumb,
And every bird and beast took part in the scene.
Here we learned the joys of the peaceable kingdom.

I see it now, an illuminated page.
The assiduous monk in his joy did not spare
Costly vermilion and gold, nor the rich sage.
He painted a garden haunting as a prayer
Where children rest still in long revery.
Stay, precious light on the snow-white peony!

A Child's Japan

1

Before we could call
America home,
In the days of exile,
My image of holiness
Was Kobo Daïshi,
Young and beautiful,
Sitting on his lotus
In a thin gold circle
Of light.
He is with me still.

My father loved
Monasteries,
His fantasy, perhaps,
To abandon wife and child
And withdraw to a cell
Or an austere pavilion
With paper walls.

From my bed
Down the long dark hall
I could see him
Circled in light,
His back always bent
Over his desk,
Motionless for hours.

My mother
Treated flowers as individuals,
Hated clutter and confusion,
Invented marvelous games—
Paper skaters
Blown across a lacquer tray—
Knew how to make a small room
Open and quiet.

We lived in austere style
Through necessity

And because it suited us,
An artist, a scholar,
And their one child.
How Japanese the rain looked
In Cambridge,
Slanting down in autumn!
How Japanese, the heavy snow in lumps
On the black branches!

It is clear to me now
That we were all three
A little in love with Japan.

2

When I flew out into the huge night,
Bearing with me a freight of memory,
My parents were dead.

I was going toward
All they had left behind
In the houses where we had lived,
In the artful measure
And sweet austerity
Of their lives—
That extravagance of work
And flowers,
Of work and music,
Of work and faith.

I was flying home to Japan—
A distant relative,
Familiar, strange,
And full of magic.

The First Autumn

For E.M.S.

Though in a little while
You will be dead again
After this first rehearsal
Since then and all the pain,
Still it's not death that spends
So tenderly this treasure
In leaf-rich golden winds,
But life in lavish measure.

October spends the aster,
Riches of purple, blue,
Lavender, white, that glow
In ragged starry cluster.
Then, when November comes,
Shaggy chrysanthemums,
Salmon-pink, saffron yellow,
All coppers bright and mellow,
Stand up against the frost
And never count the cost.

No, it's not death this year
Since then and all the pain.
It's life we harvest here
(Sun on the crimson vine).
The garden speaks your name.
We drink your joys like wine.

First Snow

This is the first soft snow
That tiptoes up to your door
As you sit by the fire and sew,
That sifts through a crack in the floor
And covers your hair with hoar.

This is the stiffening wound
Burning the heart of a deer
Chased by a moon-white hound,
This is the hunt and the queer
Sick beating of feet that fear.

This is the crisp despair
Lying close to the marrow,
Fallen out of the air
Like frost on the narrow
Bone of a shot sparrow.

This is the love that will seize
Savagely onto your mind
And do whatever he please,
This the despair, and a moon-blind
Hound you will never bind.

The House in Winter

The house in winter creaks like a ship.
Snow-locked to the sills and harbored snug
In soft white meadows, it is not asleep.
When icicles pend on the low roof's lip,
The shifting weight of a slow-motion tug
May slide off sometimes in a crashing slip.
At zero I have heard a nail pop out
From clapboard like a pistol shot.

All day this ship is sailing out on light:
At dawn we wake to rose and amber meadows,
At noon plunge on across the waves of white,
And, later, when the world becomes too bright,
Tack in among the lengthening blue shadows
To anchor in black-silver pools of night.
Although we do not really come and go,
It feels a long way up and down from zero.

At night I am aware of life aboard.
The scampering presences are often kind,
Leaving under a cushion a seed-hoard,
But I can never open any cupboard
Without a question: what shall I find?
A hard nut in my boot? An apple cored?
The house around me has become an ark
As we go creaking on from dark to dark.

There is a wilder solitude in winter
When every sense is pricked alive and keen
For what may pop or tumble down or splinter.
The light itself, as active as a painter,
Swashes bright flowing banners down
The flat white walls. I stand here like a hunter
On the *qui vive*, though all appears quite calm,
And feel the silence gather like a storm.

March-Mad

The strangely radiant skies have come
To lift us out of winter's gloom,
A paler more transparent blue,
A softer gold light on fresh snow.
It is a naked time that bares
Our slightly worn-down hopes and cares,
And sets us listening for frogs,
And sends us to seed catalogues
To bury our starved eyes and noses
In an extravagance of roses,
And order madly at this season
When we have had enough of reason.

Mud Season

In early spring, so much like a late autumn,
Gray stubble and the empty trees,
We must contend with an unwieldy earth.
In this rebirth that feels so much like dying,
When the bare patches bleed into raw mud,
In rain, in coarsening ooze, we have grown sluggard,
Cold to the marrow with spring's nonarrival:
To hold what we must hold is iron-hard,
And strength is needed for the mere survival.

By dogged labor we must learn to lift
Ourselves and bring a season in;
No one has ever called child-bearing easy,
And this spring-bearing also asks endurance.
We are strained hard within our own becoming,
Forced to learn ways how to renew, restore.
Though we were dazzled once by perfect snow,
What we have not has made us what we are.
Those surface consolations have to go.

In early spring, so much a fall of will,
We struggle through muds of unreason,
We dig deep into caring and contention;
The cold unwieldy earth resists the spade.
But we contend to bring a difficult birth
Out from the lack of talent, partial scope,
And every failure of imagination.
Science and art and love still be our hope!
What we are not drives us to consummation.

Easter Morning

The extreme delicacy of this Easter morning
Spoke to me as a prayer and as a warning.
It was light on the brink, spring light
After a rain that gentled my dark night.
I walked through landscapes I had never seen
Where the fresh grass had just begun to green,
And its roots, watered deep, sprung to my tread;
The maples wore a cloud of feathery red,
But flowering trees still showed their clear design
Against the pale blue brightness chilled like wine.
And I was praying all the time I walked,
While starlings flew about, and talked, and talked.
Somewhere and everywhere life spoke the word.
The dead trees woke; each bush held its bird.
I prayed for delicate love and difficult,
That all be gentle now and know no fault,
That all be patient—as a wild rabbit fled
Sudden before me. Dear love, I would have said
(And to each bird who flew up from the wood),
I would be gentler still if that I could,
For on this Easter morning it would seem
The softest footfall danger is, extreme . . .
And so I prayed to be less than the grass
And yet to feel the Presence that might pass.
I made a prayer. I heard the answer, "Wait,
When all is so in peril, and so delicate!"

Metamorphosis

Always it happens when we are not there—
The tree leaps up alive into the air,
Small open parasols of Chinese green
Wave on each twig. But who has ever seen
The latch sprung, the bud as it burst?
Spring always manages to get there first.

Lovers of wind, who will have been aware
Of a faint stirring in the empty air,
Look up one day through a dissolving screen
To find no star, but this multiplied green,
Shadow on shadow, singing sweet and clear.
Listen, lovers of wind, the leaves are here!

Apple Tree in May

"But it's falling already,
Falling!" I cried,
"So fast and so soon . . ."
The flowering bride
Of the white May moon.

My neighbor and I
Stood there by the door,
Petals floating down
For a moment more
On the green and the brown.

Then the boy at my side
Whom I hardly know
Said, "The petals leave"
(As he turned to go)
"But you mustn't grieve.

For they fall, you know,
To make the fruit
For the harvest moon:
Don't you be put out
So fast, so soon."

It was falling already,
Falling, my joy,
So fast and so soon,
When a country boy
Said, "The harvest moon . . ."

A Glass of Water

Here is a glass of water from my well.
It tastes of rock and root and earth and rain;
It is the best I have, my only spell,
And it is cold, and better than champagne.
Perhaps someone will pass this house one day
To drink, and be restored, and go his way,
Someone in dark confusion as I was
When I drank down cold water in a glass,
Drank a transparent health to keep me sane,
After the bitter mood had gone again.

A Flower-Arranging Summer

The white walls of this airy house assume
Flowers as natural and needed friends;
All summer long while flowers are in bloom
Attentive expectation never ends.
The day begins with walking through wet grass
In a slow progress, to visit the whole garden,
And all is undecided as I pass,
For here I must be thief and also warden:
What must I leave? What can I bear to plunder?
What fragile freshness, what amazing throat
Has opened in the night, what single wonder
That will be sounded like a single note,
When these light wandering thoughts deploy
Before the grave deeds of decisive joy?

Later, I cut judiciously and fill my basket.
It's a fine clamor of unrelated voices,
As I begin the day's adventure and slow task,
The delicate, absorbing task of choices—
That lavender and pink that need some acid,
Perhaps a saffron zinnia, linen-crisp?
Or poppy's crinkle beside the rich and placid
Rose petal, and some erratic plume or wisp
To enhance cosmos, its flat symmetry,
And always the poised starry phlox in masses—
Sometimes I have undone the same bouquet
A dozen times in six different glasses,
A dozen times and still dissatisfied,
As if that day my wish had been denied.

Sometimes two poppies can compose a world,
Two and one seed-pagoda on a hairy stem,
Blood-red, vermilion, each entity unfurled
Clashes its cymbals in the silent room;
The scale so small, substance diaphanous,
Yet the reverberation of that twofold red
Has focused one room for me ever since,
As if an Absolute had once been said.
Sometimes the entire morning does get lost

In ochers, greenish-whites, in warm deep rose,
As I pick all the zinnias against frost,
Salmon, crude red, magenta—and who knows
What harsh loud chords of music sweep the room?
Both chords and discords, till the whole bright thing
Explodes into a brilliant cloud of bloom,
And the white walls themselves begin to sing.

And so the morning's gone. Was this to waste it
In a long foolish flowery meditation?
Time slides away, and how are we to taste it?
Within the floating world all is sensation.
And yet I see eternity's long wink
In these elusive games, and only there:
When I can so suspend myself to think,
I seem suspended in undying air.

Sun Boat

As if this light boat had no keel,
As if the mast carried no sail,
With no hand on the tiller to guide
The gentle rocking, the glide,

It swings up floated upon air,
And never changeable wind there,
Only the lightest little motion,
That ripple on the pulse of ocean,

As the sun breathes in stillness, weaves
The warmth in slowly rising waves.
And if the boat seems strangely gifted,
It is that it is being lifted.

The mariner has yielded will
And given to the sun his skill,
And lost his course in summer air
Content to be a passenger.

The Fig

Under the green leaf hangs a little pouch
Shaped like a gourd, purple and leathery.
It fits the palm, it magnetizes touch.
What flesh designed as fruit can this fruit be?

The plump skin gives a little at the seam.
Now bite it deep for better or for worse!
Oh multitude of stars, pale green and crimson—
And you have dared to eat a universe!

The Olive Grove

Here in the olive grove,
Under the cobalt dome,
The ancient spirits move
And light comes home,

And nests in silvery leaves.
It makes each branch a cloud,
And comes and goes, and weaves
Aerial song aloud.

Here every branch is gifted
With spiritual fruit
And every leaf is lifted
To brightness from the root.

Where the terrestrial plane
Meets vision and desire,
The silver and the green
Are strung on a great lyre,

And leafy seraphim
The sun and shade among
Turn each grove to a hymn;
Whole hillsides are in song.

Silvery, shadowy now
The fruit over our head,
Who lie and hardly know
which is light, which is bread.

To the North

We have come back to the cold North,
Come home after the passionate going forth,
After the olive groves, the Alpine meadow,
The purple seas under a mountain shadow,
The rich and crumbling ruins in the hills
Those storms of light in the psychic cathedrals.
After the passionate summer going forth,
We have come back to the cold North.

We have come at the year's turning,
Before the leaves fall, when the leaves are burning,
Before the apples, the late roses, fall,
When all is empty and yet bountiful.
We have cried "Beauty, Beauty!" up and down,
But that restless pursuit is overthrown,
And Beauty turned to ashes in the mouth,
Consumed by the consuming South.

Oh splendid was that spendthrift living,
The quick growth in the South, the overgiving,
But ripeness tumbles swiftly into ruin
And death is there under that awful sun,
The fig bursting with sweetness, the grape broken,
And every word too heavy that is spoken—
And we come back now, silenced, to this earth
To bind up selfhood in the North.

A Guest

My woods belong to woodcock and to deer;
For them, it is an accident I'm here.

If, for the plump raccoon, I represent
An ash can that was surely heaven-sent,

The bright-eyed mask, the clever little paws
Obey not mine, but someone else's laws.

The young buck takes me in with a long glance
That says that I, not he, am here by chance.

And they all go their ways, as I must do,
Up through the green and down again to snow,

No one of us responsible or near,
But each himself and in the singular.

When we do meet, I am the one to stare
As if an angel had me by the hair,

As I am flooded by some ancient bliss
Before all I possess and can't possess.

So when a stranger knocks hard at the door,
He cannot know what I am startled for—

To see before me an unfurry face,
A creature like myself in this wild place.

Our wilderness gets wilder every day
And we intend to keep the tamed at bay.

The Metaphysical Garden

I

It was late in September when you took me
To that amazing garden, hidden in the city,
Tranquil and complicated as an open hand,
There among green pleasances and descant of fountains,
Through walled paths and dappled loggias
Opening to distant trees,
We went conversing, smoking, often silent,
Our feet cool in sandals, nonchalant as the air.

It was at the end of September, warm for the season.
Nothing had fallen yet to bruise the grass.
Ripeness was all suspended,
The air aromatic and fresh over sun-drenched box.

Critical as Chinese philosophers,
We performed the garden by easy stages:
Should we move toward shade or toward sunlight,
The closed dark pool or the panoplied fountain?
Clearly each path had a metaphysical meaning,
Those rustic steps, that marble balustrade.
It was late in September when time,
Time that is not ours,
Hid itself away.

II

Our first arrival was a square room,
Brilliant parquet of clover
Designed as a stage for the trees
And their subtle conversations,
Diapason of faintly stirring leaves;
The fountains, heard not seen,
Made silence crepitant aand watery.
And here it seemed we were part of a discourse
On the ancient themes,
Perspective and enclosure,
Desire raised and fulfilled
To this complex alive composure.

It was there that your voice,
Harsh and aloof,
Mixed with the cry of a bird
As a cardinal flashed through the willow
And suddenly screamed.

III

We climbed lightly
Through a small steep orchard
To a bastion of branches.
Must we penetrate, force passage
At the top of the hill?
No airy place, no view?

What we found was a grave high room,
Lonely, enclosed in acacias,
Its center a double pool
Where ivy crept and crowded
And water lilies slept, going to seed.
We had not after all expected
A place so perfectly round.
We sat on a stone bench like statues.
Nothing moved.

Nothing moved for a long season.
From high in the sunlight then
A single leaf fell slowly,
And we watched it fall.
So passionate was the place, so still,
This light leaf falling from air to grass
Was monumental. It held
The exact weight of a tremendous word.

IV

How gentle and relieving
Then to emerge, climb down
From that intense enclosure
High on the hill
To the large view we had imagined

Through all the devious paths,
The orchards, loggias,
The long boxed-in perspectives.

Now it was here,
The weight of the trees flung back,
The undulating ample slopes,
The whole shape of the land
Made clear in the golden light.
In the foreground tawny dogwood
Thick with vermilion berries, showed
Brilliantly sharp.
We could read each leaf.

We had to climb down
To get to contemplation
On this scale, large, airy, remote.
We sat on a homely wooden bench
And watched a solitary gardener pass
With his pruning hook.
Indeed it was coming home
To an unbroken sunlit peace of knowing.

Of the Seasons

Sangre de Cristo Mountains
Sante Fe, New Mexico

You spoke of spring and summer
As we drove through the pinyon-spotted
Through the leopard-land, the hammer
Of sun on the bronze and the violet.
You spoke of lilies brushing
The horses' necks in spring
And dry creeks water-rushing,
"In the spring," you told me.

I remember all that you said
Of the sharp cleavage, the heat,
The cold that makes the head
Burn with an inner tension,
Sound like a glass humming.
Words break in crystal air
And silence is always coming,
"It is here," you told me.

And when you spoke of summer,
I knew the heat is in waves
And earth begins to shimmer
With violent reds and umber.
On the naked rock you told
How the fierce path of wind
Burned the structure bright as gold,
And rock fire-bare not barren,
"In the summer," you told me.

We did not speak of winter
For then we turned and saw
The sun crash and then splinter
On peaks till they were flooded
With light that aches with rose,
And all the mountains iced
Are burned again—"and those,"
You said, "are called The Blood of Christ."

Bears and Waterfalls

Kind kinderpark
For bear buffoons
And fluid graces—
Who dreamed this lark
Of spouts, lagoons,
And huge fur faces?

For bears designed
Small nooks, great crags,
And Gothic mountains?
For bears refined
Delightful snags,
Waterfalls, fountains?

Who had the wit to root
A forked tree where a sack
Of honey plumps on end,
A rich-bottomed fruit
To rouse a hearty whack
From passing friend?

Who ever did imagine
A waterspout as stool,
Or was black bear the wiser
Who sat down on this engine
To keep a vast rump cool.
Then, cooled, set free a geyser?

Who dreamed a great brown queen
Sleeked down in her rough silk
Flirting with her huge lord,
Breast-high in her tureen?—
"Splash me, delightful hulk!"
So happy and absurd.

Bear upside-down, white splendor,
All creamy, foaming fur,
And childhood's rug come true,
All nonchalance and candor,
Black pads your signature—
Who, above all, dreamed you?

When natural and formal
Are seen to mate so well,
Where bears and fountains play,
Who would return to normal?
Go back to human Hell?
Not I. I mean to stay,

To hold this happy chance
Forever in the mind,
To be where waters fall
And archetypes still dance,
As they were once designed
In Eden for us all.

The Puritan

Once he was seduced by the soft luxurious hill,
The peace-inducing landscape, interminably green,
Where rivers are shallow, full of flowers and still,
Where the rain is gentle, falling without spleen.

Today he thinks of bare pastures and cedar trees,
The bitter land where a child is hardy and learns
To be fearful of his heart, to be wary of what he feels
Hiding among the juniper bushes and the brown ferns.

He remembers the stone walls marking field from field,
Piled up out of infinite stones by the patient hand,
He thinks of the thin harvest that those pastures yield,
How the men are lean men, how it is a stern land.

He thinks of a country where roots are durable and deep,
Where the speech has a tang in it and is never mild,
Where the kind of peace is the snow coming sometimes like sleep,
So cold it would freeze up the tears of a soft child.

V

In a Dirty Time

The war games are over,
And all the laurel's gone.
Dead warrior, dead lover,
Was the war lost or won?
What say you, blasted head?
No answer from the dead.

"We'll to the Woods No More . . ."

from *To The Living*

III

How faint the horn sounds in the mountain passes
Where, folded in the folds of memory,
All the heroic helmets lie in summer grasses,
Who wore them vanished utterly.

How dry the blood on ancient cross and stone
Where, folded in the folds of memory,
The martyrs cry out where each falls alone
In his last faithful agony.

How fresh and clear the stains of human weeping
Where, folded in the folds of memory,
The millions who have died for us are sleeping
In our long tragic history.

Stone Walls

They make me wince, such vivid dreams rise up
When I walk second growth and witness spill
Tumbled by roots, with no one there to keep
Stones balanced or to care whether the wall
Stays firm or not. But truth is, after all,
They were not built for walls so much as dumps
For the waste stuff the glacier left behind.
Farmers have fought this land of rocky bumps
For two long centuries, always to find
Daily frustration of a cussèd kind
Where clever men gave up for lack of hope.
Some heroes piled the walls, saw thick-wooled sheep
Cropping at last on the rough grassy slope.
It looked like hard-won riches that would keep—
Until Australia came in on the cheap,
To ruin all that they had labored for
Those cruel years before the Civil War.

I wince, and then I feel a kind of pride.
Those who left, left to find the easy plain.
Those who stayed learned to grow some rock inside,
To build hard substance out of loss and pain,
Start thinking fresh, endure and contain.
Those who stayed either grew ingenious
Or degenerate—the pivot, mind.
Stark need fostered inventive genius.
Mills, factories of every kind
Sprang from that losing fight against the land.

Although I came here from a different waste—
The fertile fields war crossed and recrossed
(England and Belgium married in my past)—
I feel like memory itself these pastures lost,
And wince at what the broken stone walls cost.

Monticello

This legendary house, this dear enchanted tomb,
Once so supremely lived in, and for life designed,
Will none of moldy death nor give it room,
Charged with the presence of a living mind.

Enter, and touch the temper of a lively man.
See, it is spacious, intimate and full of light.
The eye, pleased by detail, is nourished by the plan;
Nothing is here for show, much for delight.

All the joys of invention and of craft and wit,
Are freely granted here, all given rein,
But taut within the classic form and ruled by it,
Elegant, various, magnificent—and plain,

Europe become implacably American!
Yet Mozart could have been as happy here,
As Monroe riding from his farm again,
As well as any silversmith or carpenter—

As well as we, for whom this elegance,
This freedom in a form, this peaceful grace,
Is not our heritage, although it happened once:
We read the future, not the past, upon his face.

The time must come when, from the people's heart,
Government grows to meet the stature of a man,
And freedom finds its form, that great unruly art,
And the state is a house designed by Jefferson.

Charleston Plantations

You cannot see them from the road: go far and deep,
Down the long avenues where mosses cover up the leaves,
Across the empty terraced lawns neglected and asleep,
To the still place where no dog barks and no dove grieves,
And a black mirror gives you back your face too white
In pools dyed jet by cypress roots: go deep and far,
Deep into time, far into crumbling spaces and half-light
To where they stand, our Egypt and our Nineveh.
Deep in a deathly stillness stand the planters' houses.

The garlands and the little foxes' faces carved
Upon the mantels look on empty walls and water-stains
And the stairs tremble though so elegantly curved
(Outside are waiting the bright creeping vines),
And as your foot falls in the silences, you guess
Decay has been arrested for a moment in the wall,
But the gray plumes upon the trees in deathly loveliness
Will stir when you have passed, and somewhere a stone fall.
Deep in a deathly stillness stand the planters' houses.

There is no rice now and the world that sprang from it
Like an azalea, brilliant from the swamps, has crumbled.
A single century, it is embalmed as Egypt.
A single century, and all that elegance was humbled—
While we who fired that world and watched it burn
Come every spring to whisper near the tomb,
To stare, a little shaken, where the mosses mourn
And the azaleas and magnolias have not ceased to bloom.
Deep in a deathly stillness stand the planters' houses.

Who Wakes

Detroit, June 1943

Who wakes now who lay blind with sleep?
Who starts bright-eyed with anger from his bed?
I do. I, the plain citizen. I cannot sleep.
I hold the torturing fire in my head.

I, an American, call the dead Negro's name,
And in the hot dark of the city night
I walk the streets alone and sweat with shame.
Too late to rise, to raise the dead too late.

This is the harvest. The seeds sown long ago—
The careless word, sly thought, excusing glance.
I reap now everything I let pass, let go.
This is the harvest of my own indifference.

I, the plain citizen, have grown disorder
In my own world. It is not what I meant.
But dreams and images are potent and can murder.
I stand accused of them. I am not innocent.

Can I now plant imagination, honesty,
And love, where violence and terror were unbound—
The images of hope, the dream's responsibility?

Those who died here were murdered in my mind.

The Tortured

Cried Innocence, "Mother, my thumbs, my thumbs!
The pain will make me wild."
And Wisdom answered, "Your brother-man
Is suffering, my child."

Screamed Innocence, "Mother, my eyes, my eyes!
Someone is blinding me."
And Wisdom answered, "Those are your brother's eyes,
The blinded one is he."

Cried Innocence, "Mother, my heart, my heart!
It bursts with agony."
And Wisdom answered, "That is your brother's heart
Breaking upon a tree."

Screamed Innocence, "Mother, I want to die.
I cannot bear the pain."
And Wisdom answered, "They will not let him die.
They bring him back again."

Cried Innocence, "Mother, I cannot bear
It now. My flesh is wild!"
And Wisdom answered, "His agony is endless
For your sake, my child."

Then whispered Innocence, "Mother, forgive
Forgive my sin, forgive—"
And Wisdom wept. "Now do you understand, Love,
How you must live?"

Night Watch

1

Sweet night nursing a neighbor—
The old lady lifts her hands
And writes a message
On the air—
Gently I lay them down.
Sudden motion
Might shift the bandage
Over one eye.

Across the hall
A woman moans twice.
I alone am not in pain,
Wide-awake under a circle of light.

Two days ago in Kentucky
I was the sick child,
Sick for this patchy, barren earth,
For tart talk,
Dissatisfaction,
Sharp bitter laughter,
Sick for a granite pillow.

Among that grass soft as silk,
Those courtesies, those evasions,
I was sick as a trout
In a stagnant pond.

Wide-awake,
I weigh one thing against another.
The old lady will see
Better than before;
The woman who moaned
Sleeps herself whole again.

Sweet, innocent night
In the hospital
Where wounds can be healed!

2

The birds sing
Before dawn,
And before dawn
I begin to see a little.
I hold the old warm hand in mine
To keep it from clawing
The bandage,
And to comfort me.

I am happy as a mother
Whose good baby sleeps.

In Kentucky
They are spurned mothers,
Curse the children
And their hot black eyes,
Hard from not weeping;
Remember the old days,
Dear pickaninnies,
Mouths pink as watermelon.

What happens
When the baby screams,
Batters the barred cage of its bed,
Wears patience thin?

What happens
When the baby is six feet tall,
Throws stones,
Breaks windows?

What happens
When the grown man
Beats out against us
His own hard core,
Wants to hurt?

In the white night
At the hospital
I listened hard.
I weighed one thing

Against another.
I heard, "Love, love."
(Love them to death?)

And at dawn I heard a voice,
"If you love them,
Let them grow."

3

The convalescent
Is quick to weak rage
Or tears;
In a state of growth
We are in pain,
Violent, hard to live with.
Our wounds ache.
We curse rather than bless.

4

"I hate them," she said.
"They spoil everything," said
The woman from Baltimore.
"It is not the dear old town
I used to know."

I felt pain like an assault,
The old pain again
When the world thrusts itself inside,
When we have to take in the outside,
When we have to decide
To be crazy-human with hope
Or just plain crazy
With fear.

(The drunken black in the subway
Will rape you, white woman,
Because you had bad dreams.)

Stomach pain, or vomit it.
In Kentucky I threw up
One whole night.
Get rid of this great sick baby

We carry around
Or go through the birth-sweat again.
Lazy heart,
Slow self-indulgent beat,
Take the sick world in.

5

In Baltimore
The black who drove me to the airport
Seemed an enormous, touchable
Blessing.
"When you give a speech," he told me,
"And you get that scared feeling,
Take a deep breath. It helps."

Comfort flowed out from him.
He talked about pain
In terms of healing.
Of Baltimore, that great hospital
Where the wounds fester
Among azaleas and dogwood,
The lovely quiet gardens,
"We are making things happen,"
Said the black man.
"It is going to be beautiful."
He had no doubt.

Wide awake in the hospital
In the morning light,
I weighed one thing against the other.
I took a deep breath.

Easter, 1968

Now we have buried the face we never knew,
Now we have silenced the voice we never heard,
Now he is dead we look on him with awe . . .
Dead king, dear martyr, and anointed Word.
Where thousands followed, each must go home
Into his secret heart and learn the pain,
Stand there on rock and, utterly alone,
Come to terms with this burning suffering man;
Torn by his hunger from our fat and greed,
And bitten by his thirst from careless sloth,
Must wake, inflamed, to answer for his blood
With the slow-moving inexorable truth
That we can earn even a moment's balm
Only with acts of caring, and fierce calm.

Head of an African, vital and young,
The full lips fervent as an open rose,
The high-domed forehead full of light and strong—
Look on this man again. The blood still flows.
Listen once more to the impassioned voice
Till we are lifted on his golden throat
And trumpet-call of agony and choice
Out of our hesitating shame and doubt.
Remember how he prayed before the task.
Remember how he walked, eyes bright and still,
Unarmed, his bronze face shining like a mask,
Through stones and curses, hatred hard as hail.
Now we have silenced the voice we never heard,
Break open, heart, and listen to his word.

"We'll to the Woods No More, the Laurels Are Cut Down"

At Kent State

The war games are over,
The laurels all cut down.
We'll to the woods no more
With live ammunition
To murder our own children
Because they hated war.

The war games are over.
How many times in pain
We were given a choice—
"Sick of the violence"
(Oh passionate human voice!)—
But buried it again.

The war games are over.
Virile, each stood alone—
John, Robert, Martin Luther.
Still we invoke the gun,
Still make a choice for murder,
Bury the dead again.

The war games are over,
And all the laurel's gone.
Dead warrior, dead lover,
Was the war lost or won?
What say you, blasted head?
No answer from the dead.

Ballad of the Sixties

In the West of the country where I was
Hoping for some good news,
Only the cripple had fire,
Only the cripple knew the mind's desire;
In the wheel chair alone
Poetry met the eyes
That see and recognize,
There in the wizened bone.
    For only the ill are well,
    And only the mad are sane.
    This is the sad truth plain,
    The story I have to tell.

In the North of the country where I saw
The anxious rich and the angry poor,
Only the blasted life had reason;
Only the stricken in the bitter season
Looked out of loss and learned
The waste of all that burned,
Once cared and burned.
    For only the mad are sane,
    And only the lost are well,
    And loss of fire the bane
    Of this season in Hell.

In the South of the country where I passed
Looking for faith and hope at last,
Only the black man knew
The false dream from the true;
Only the dark and grieving
Could be the still believing.
    For only the ill are well,
    Only the hunted, free,
    So the story I have to tell
    In the South was told to me.

In the East of the country where I came
Back to my house, back to my name,
Only the crazy girl was clear

That all has been betrayed to fear;
Only the mad girl knew the cost,
And she, shut up from wind and rain
And safely plucked out from her pain,
Knew that our love is lost, is lost.
 For only the sick are well;
 The mad alone have truth to tell
 In the mad games they play—
 Our love has withered away.

Letter from Chicago

For Virginia Woolf

Four years ago I met your death here,
Heard it where I had never been before
In a city of departures, streets of wind,
Soft plumes of smoke dissolving—
City of departures beside an aloof lake.
Here where you never were, they said,
"Virginia Woolf is dead."

The city died. I died in the city,
Witness of unreal tears, my own,
For experience involves time
And time was gone
The world arrested at the instant of death.
I wept wildly like a child
Who cannot give his present after all:
I met your death and did not recognize you.

Now you are dead four years
And there are no more private tears.
The city of departure is the city of arrival,
City of triumphant wind lifting people,
City of spring: yesterday I found you.
Wherever I looked was love.
Wherever I went I had presents in my hands.
Wherever I went I recognized you.

You are not, never to be again,
Never, never to be dead,
Never to be dead again in this city,
Never to be mourned again,
But to come back yearly,
Hourly, with the spring, with the wind,
Fresh as agony or resurrection;
A plume of smoke dissolving,
Remaking itself, never still,
Never static, never lost:
The place where time flows again.

I speak to you and meet my own life.
Is it to be poised as the lake beside the city,
Aloof, but given still to air and wind,
Detached from time, but given to the moment—
Is it to be a celebration always?

I send you love forward into the past.

The Ballad of Johnny

(A News Item)

For safety on the expedition
A name-tag on each child was hung,
A necklace-name, his very own,
So he could not get lost for long.

Johnny jumped up and down for joy
To have a name forever true.
"I'm Johnny," cried the little boy.
"Johnny is going to the zoo!"

"Johnny," he whispered in the subway.
His whole face was suffused with bliss.
This was the best, the greatest day.
Boldly he gave his name a kiss.

But soon forgot it at the zoo
And let the name-tag swing out free,
For could that elephant be true?
And there was so much to see . . .

Look, Johnny, at the monkey swinging
High in the air on his trapeze!
He heard the gibbon's sharp shrill singing
And begged to hold the monkey, please.

Then saw a goat and ran off fast
To hug the dear fantastic thing,
An animal to stroke at last,
A living toy for all his loving.

The soft lips nibbled at his sweater
And Johnny laughed with joy to feel
Such new-found friendliness and, better,
To know this animal was real.

His face was breathing in fur coat,
He did not notice anything
As gentle lips and greedy throat
Swallowed the name-tag and the string.

But when he found that they were gone
And he had lost his name for good,
Dreadful it was to be alone,
And Johnny screamed his terror loud.

The friendly goat was strange and wild,
And the cold eyes' indifferent stare
Could give no comfort to the child
Who had become No one, Nowhere.

"I've lost my name. I'm going to die,"
He shouted when his teacher came
And found him too afraid to cry.
"But, Johnny, you still have your name!

"It's not a tag, it's in your head,
And you are Johnny through and through.
Look in the mirror," teacher said,
"There's Johnny looking out at you."

But he had never had a mirror,
And Johnny met there a strange child
And screamed dismay at this worse error,
And only grew more lost and wild.

"No, no," he screamed, "that's is not me,
That ugly boy I don't know who . . ."
Great treasure lost, identity,
When a goat ate it at the zoo.

A Recognition

For Perley Cole

I wouldn't know how rare they come these days,
But I know Perley's rare. I know enough
To stop fooling around with words, and praise
This man who swings a scythe in subtle ways,
And brings green order, carved out of the rough.
I wouldn't know how rare, but I discover
They used to tell an awkward learning boy,
"Keep the heel down, son, careful of the swing!"
I guess at perils and peril makes me sing.
So let the world go, but hold fast to joy,
And praise the craftsman till Hell freezes over!

I watched him that first morning when the dew
Still slightly bent tall, toughened grasses,
Sat up in bed to watch him coming through
Holding the scythe so lightly and so true
In slow sweeps and in lovely passes,
The swing far out, far out—but not too far,
The pause to wipe and whet the shining blade.
I felt affinities: farmer and poet
Share a good deal, although they may not know it.
It looked as easy as when the world was made,
And God could pull a bird out or a star.

For there was Perley in his own sweet way
Pulling some order out of ragged land,
Cutting the tough, chaotic growth away,
So peace could saunter down a summer day,
For here comes Cole with genius in his hand!
I saw in him a likeness to that flame,
Brancusi, in his Paris studio,
Who pruned down, lifted from chaotic night
Those naked, shining images of flight—
The old man's gentle malice and bravado,
Boasting hard times: "It was my game!"

"*C'était mon jeu!*"—to wrest joy out of pain,
The endless skillful struggle to uncloud

The clouded vision, to reduce and prune,
And bring back from the furnace, fired again,
A world of magic, joy alone allowed.
Now Perley says, "God damn it!"—and much worse.
Hearing him, I get back some reverence.
Could you, they ask, call such a man your friend?
Yes (damn it!), and yes world without end!
Brancusi's game and his make the same sense,
And not unlike a prayer is Perley's curse.

So let the rest go, and heel down, my boy,
And praise the artist till Hell freezes over,
For he is rare, he with his scythe (no toy),
He with his perils, with his skill and joy,
Who comes to prune, to make clear, to uncover,
The old man, full of wisdom, in his prime.
There in the field, watching him as he passes,
I recognize that violent, gentle blood,
Impatient patience. I would, if I could,
Call him my kin, there scything down the grasses,
Call him my good luck in a dirty time.

VI

Invocations and Mythologies

I tell you the gods are still alive
And they are not consoling.

"At Delphi"

I turn your face around! It is my face.
That frozen rage is what I must explore—
O secret, self-enclosed, and ravaged place!
This is the gift I thank Medusa for.

"The Muse as Medusa"

The Approach—Calcutta

1

Landing
At four o'clock in the morning,
No man's hour,
I felt only dread.

Muslims drove a herd
Of gaunt cows
To the slaughter,
While the Hindus slept,
A shrouded multitude,
On the streets.
The whole city
Appeared to be
An improvised morgue.

Even a beggar's withered hand
Stretched out, inert,
As if already dead.

2

Here the gods themselves
Are too thick, too many,
Turn themselves into snakes,
Fish, or even boars,
And into sinuous lovers
Twined,
Erotic and restless,
In the coils of the eternal dance

Hot winds blew me
Hither and thither;
Barren,
Clouded by ignorance,
I peered out
At an impenetrable world:
People, animals,
Earth, gods,
Who none of them smiled.

Notes from India

The letters ask:
You describe so much,
But how do you feel?
What is happening to you?
What I see is happening to me.

1. *At Bhubaneswar*

The ragged, rough, continental spaces
Where people never stop walking,
Alone or in long lines,
Over the dirt roads
Under hot, windy skies—
Dark figures walking
With the air of pilgrims
In saris faded
Purple, soft red, dark blue;
Clerks in white dhoties
Carrying black umbrellas,
Barefoot, erect;
Old men in dusty turbans
Naked to the waist;
Women carrying jugs on their heads;
Children in bright yellow and pink;
And, against the horizon,
Four carts and their bullocks
Walking, walking.
It has no beginning. It never ends.

Hunching themselves toward the sky,
Lifting the earth with them,
These temples seem to be waiting
For something that happened
Nine centuries ago.
Inside, the rough phallus stands erect;
Outside, the sculptured lovers embrace,
While black kites
Float on the sullen air,

And the world stands still,
An everlasting noon.

The fresh watercolor
Green of rice,
A flight of emerald parakeets,
The kingfisher's radiant blue—
Among the dead colors,
The cracked dry fields,
They meet the eye
As if earth burst
Like a pomegranate
To show its brilliance,
Fecundity of light.

The woman in a red sari,
Standing, thin presence
Among dessicated fields,
To watch us pass,
Looks as if she alone
Supported the whole sky.

In the temple pond
A young man prays
With folded hands,
His bronze chest bare
As he stands up to his waist
In the filthy, promiscuous,
Healing water.
Old women gossip under the banyan tree
While a Brahmin
Circumnavigates
The whitewashed temple
Chanting the morning prayer.
Little girls,
Damp hair stuck to their foreheads,
Dress in clean dresses—
The pool is troubled
Again and again
By the dark bodies

That go down through the scum
And return to the morning,
Smiling the smile of the newly washed.
In the distance a dove
Repeats itself.

I had been the woman
With a camera eye
Who notices everything
And is always watched,
The stranger on whom
No one smiled.
Then I slipped,
Fell headlong
In the red dust,
And at once the rickshaw boy
Is there at my side.
Thin expert hands
Feel hard for a break,
Then wipe the blood off
With a filthy cloth.
Worth a scraped knee
To land on this earth at last,
To be helped alive,
To be, in fact,
Touched!
The unsmiling people
Throng around me,
Smiling their pleasure.
Yes, I have landed.
Yes, I am alive.

2. *At Kanarak*

Out of the huge stone fortress,
Crouching within its four gates
And slowly sinking into the sand
With all its embracing figures,
Boring erotica,
Hourly more earthbound,
Caught on the wheel—

My field glasses
Suddenly caught
The smile of the Sun God—
A fleeting second,
But hours later
I was still
Under his spell.

3. *At Puri*

In the late afternoon sun
The Rajah's mildewed palaces,
Deep rose and ocher,
Sleep on the sands
Like couchant beasts,
Their eyes closed.
Where are the Rajahs now?

Three women:
We see their bare feet
Under the swinging door.
What are they up to
Behind the shutters
Of the hotel porch
In the burning afternoon?
At intervals
One lifts a hand with a duster,
Then lets it fall.
It takes much longer,
Apparently,
To do nothing
Than to do something
In air so heavy
It might be sand
Before the monsoon.

The Lord Jaganath
Brings to this sleepy city by the sea
The faces of all India.
Young ladies
In steel-rimmed glasses

Look studiously out
On this congregation:
Widows in white saris,
Those opulent balloons;
Mud-encrusted sadhus,
Sacred cows,
Fishermen and monkeys;
Black women with gold ornaments
In their nostrils;
Fine-featured Brahmins—
There is no end to the differences,
To the staggering variety
Among the pilgrims.

But when they go down to the sands
To be purified
They are a single pink and white wave
Going out together
To meet the multitudinous sea.

4. *At Fathpur Sikri*

Where once the Moghul princes
Rode with falcons on their wrists,
An old man
Sings a song
To make two monkeys dance.

The Invocation to Kali

. . . The Black Goddess Kali, the terrible one of many names, "difficult of approach," whose stomach is a void and so can never be filled, and whose womb is giving birth forever to all things . . .
Joseph Campbell

1

There are times when
I think only of killing
The voracious animal
Who is my perpetual shame,

The violent one
Whose raging demands
Break down peace and shelter
Like a peacock's scream.

There are times when
I think only of how to do away
With this brute power
That cannot be tamed.

I am the cage where poetry
Paces and roars. The beast
Is the god. How murder the god?
How live with the terrible god?

2

The Kingdom of Kali

Anguish is always there, lurking at night,
Wakes us like a scourge, the creeping sweat
As rage is remembered, self-inflicted blight.
What is it in us we have not mastered yet?

What Hell have we made of the subtle weaving
Of nerve with brain, that all centers tear?
We live in a dark complex of rage and grieving.
The machine grates, grates, whatever we are.

The kingdom of Kali is within us deep.
The built-in destroyer, the savage goddess,
Wakes in the dark and takes away our sleep.
She moves through the blood to poison gentleness.

She keeps us from being what we long to be;
Tenderness withers under her iron laws.
We may hold her like a lunatic, but it is she
Held down, who bloodies with her claws.

How then to set her free or come to terms
With the volcano itself, the fierce power
Erupting injuries, shrieking alarms?
Kali among her skulls must have her hour.

It is time for the invocation, to atone
For what we fear most and have not dared to face:
Kali, the destroyer, cannot be overthrown;
We must stay, open-eyed, in the terrible place.

Every creation is born out of the dark.
Every birth is bloody. Something gets torn.
Kali is there to do her sovereign work
Or else the living child will be stillborn.

She cannot be cast out (she is here for good)
Nor battled to the end. Who wins that war?
She cannot be forgotten, jailed, or killed.
Heaven must still be balanced against her.

Out of destruction she comes to wrest
The juice from the cactus, its harsh spine,
And until she, the destroyer, has been blest,
There will be no child, no flower, and no wine.

3

The Concentration Camps

Have we managed to fade them out like God?
Simply eclipse the unpurged images?
Eclipse the children with a mountain of shoes?
Let the bones fester like animal bones,

False teeth, bits of hair, spilled liquid eyes,
Disgusting, not to be looked at, like a blight?

Ages ago we closed our hearts to blight.
Who believes now? Who cries, "merciful God"?
We gassed God in the ovens, great piteous eyes,
Burned God in a trash heap of images,
Refused to make a compact with dead bones,
And threw away the children with their shoes—

Millions of sandals, sneakers, small worn shoes—
Thrust them aside as a disgusting blight.
Not ours, this death, to take into our bones,
Not ours a dying mutilated God.
We freed our minds from gruesome images,
Pretended we had closed their open eyes

That never could be closed, dark puzzled eyes,
The ghosts of children who went without shoes
Naked toward the ovens' bestial images,
Strangling for breath, clawing the blight,
Piled up like pigs beyond the help of God. . . .
With food in our stomachs, flesh on our bones,

We turned away from the stench of bones,
Slept with the living, drank in sexy eyes,
Hurried for shelter from a murdered God.
New factories turned out millions of shoes.
We hardly noticed the faint smell of blight,
Stuffed with new cars, ice cream, rich images.

But no grass grew on the raw images.
Corruption mushroomed from decaying bones.
Joy disappeared. The creature of the blight
Rose in the cities, dark smothered eyes.
Our children danced with rage in their shoes,
Grew up to question who had murdered God,

While we evaded their too attentive eyes,
Walked the pavane of death in our new shoes,
Sweated with anguish and remembered God.

4

The Time of Burning

For a long time, we shall have only to listen,
Not argue or defend, but listen to each other.
Let curses fall without intercession,
Let those fires burn we have tried to smother.

What we have pushed aside and tried to bury
Lives with a staggering thrust we cannot parry.

We have to reckon with Kali for better or worse,
The angry tongue that lashes us with flame
As long-held hope turns bitter and men curse,
"Burn, baby, burn" in the goddess' name.

We are asked to bear it, to take in the whole,
The long indifferent beating down of soul.

It is the time of burning, hate exposed.
We shall have to live with only Kali near.
She comes in her fury, early or late, disposed
To tantrums we have earned and must endure.

We have to listen to the harsh undertow
To reach the place where Kali can bestow.

But she must have her dreadful empire first
Until the prisons of the mind are broken free
And every suffering center at its worst
Can be appealed to her dark mystery.

She comes to purge the altars in her way,
And at her altar we shall have to pray.

It is a place of skulls, a deathly place
Where we confront our violence and feel,
Before that broken and self-ravaged face,
The murderers we are, brought here to kneel.

5

It is time for the invocation:

Kali, be with us.
Violence, destruction, receive our homage.
Help us to bring darkness into the light,
To lift out the pain, the anger,
Where it can be seen for what it is—
The balance-wheel for our vulnerable, aching love.
Put the wild hunger where it belongs,
Within the act of creation,
Crude power that forges a balance
Between hate and love.

Help us to be the always hopeful
Gardeners of the spirit
Who know that without darkness
Nothing comes to birth
As without light
Nothing flowers.

Bear the roots in mind,
You, the dark one, Kali,
Awesome power.

The Muse as Medusa

I saw you once, Medusa; we were alone.
I looked you straight in the cold eye, cold.
I was not punished, was not turned to stone—
How to believe the legends I am told?

I came as naked as any little fish,
Prepared to be hooked, gutted, caught;
But I saw you, Medusa, made my wish,
And when I left you I was clothed in thought . . .

Being allowed, perhaps, to swim my way
Through the great deep and on the rising tide,
Flashing wild streams, as free and rich as they,
Though you had power marshaled on your side.

The fish escaped to many a magic reef;
The fish explored many a dangerous sea—
The fish, Medusa, did not come to grief,
But swims still in a fluid mystery.

Forget the image: your silence is my ocean,
And even now it teems with life. You chose
To abdicate by total lack of motion,
But did it work, for nothing really froze?

It is all fluid still, that world of feeling
Where thoughts, those fishes, silent, feed and rove;
And, fluid, it is also full of healing,
For love is healing, even rootless love.

I turn your face around! It is my face.
That frozen rage is what I must explore—
Oh secret, self-enclosed, and ravaged place!
This is the gift I thank Medusa for.

At Lindos

"What are ruins to us,
The broken stones?"
They made for the sea,
These elementals
Possessed by Poseidon.
"And what is Athene?"
The sun flamed around them.
The waters were clear green.

What compelled us
To face the harsh rock?
Why did we choose
The arduous stairways?
There lay the crescent
Of white sand below us,
And the lucky swimmers.

But at last we came out,
Stood high in the white light,
And we knew you, Athene,
Goddess of light and air,
In your roofless temple,
In your white and gold.
We were pierced with knowledge.
Lucidity burned us.
What was Poseidon now,
Or the lazy swimmers?
We looked on a flat sea
As blue as lapis.
We stood among pillars
In a soaring elation.

We ran down in triumph,
Down the jagged stairways
To brag to the bathers,
But they rose up to meet us
Mysterious strangers
With salt on their eyelids,
All stupid and shining.

So it is at Lindos,
A place of many gods.

At Delphi

The site echoes
Its own huge silences

Wherever one stands,
Whatever one sees—

Narrow terror of the pass
Or its amazing throat,
Pouring an avalanche of olives
Into the blue bay.

Crags so fierce
They nearly swallow
A city of broken pillars
Or Athene's temple,
Exquisite circle,
Gentled on all sides
By silvery leaves.

Eagles floating
On high streamers of wind,
Or that raw cleft,
Deep in the rock,
Matrix
Where the oracle
Uttered her two-edged words.

Wherever one stands,
Every path leads to Fate itself:
"Speak! Speak!"

But there is no answer.

Choose the river of olives.
Choose the eagles.
Or choose to balance
All these forces,
The violent, the gentle;
Summon them like winds
Against a lifted finger.
Choose to be human.

Everyone stands here
And listens. Listens.
Everyone stands here alone.

I tell you the gods are still alive
And they are not consoling.

I have not spoken of this
For three years,
But my ears still boom.

Birthday on the Acropolis

1

In the fifth grade
We became Greeks,
Made our own chitons,
Drank homemade mead,
And carved a small Parthenon
Out of Ivory soap.
It never seemed real,
The substance too soft,
An awkward miniature.
But over these labors
Athene towered,
Life-size.
She was real enough.

She was mine, this one,
From the beginning,
Not she of the olive,
But she of the owl-eyes,
A spear in her hand.

Any day now the air would open,
Any day . . .

2

Forty years later
I was hurled to the bright rock,
Still merged with the dark,
Edgeless and melting,
The Indian ethos—
Stepped out from the plane
To stand in the Greek light
In the knife-clean air.

Too sudden, too brilliant.
Who can bear this shining?
The pitiless clarity?
Each bone felt the shock.

I was broken in two
By sheer definition:

Rock, light, air.

3

I came from the past,
From the ancient kingdoms
To this youth of my own world,
To this primary place.

I stood at the great gate
On my fiftieth birthday,
Had rounded the globe
Toward this Acropolis,
Had come round the world
Toward this one day:

O Pallas Athene,
You of the shining shield,
Give me to stand clear,
Solid as this, your rock,
Knowing no tremor.

Today, you, Pandrosos,
Who cherish the olive,
Bring from my battered trunk
The small silver leaves,
Fresh and unshielded.

Make the olives rich
In essential oil;
May the fruit fall lightly
As small drops of rain
On the parched fields.
Protect the small trees.

Today, you, Aglauros,
Pure prow of Athens,
Poise me in balance
So that all clarity
May meet all mystery
As on the spear's point.

4

When proportion triumphs,
When measure is conscious,
Who is to protect us from arrogance?

The presence of the gods. They are here:
Fate's ambiguities and jealous Athene.

No, it is not a place for youth,
This bastion where man's reason grew strong.
These pillars speak of mature power.

Imagined as white, they are rough gold,
The spaces between them open as justice
To frame mountains
And the distant, blue, world-opening sea.

5

On my fiftieth birthday I met the archaic smile.
It was the right year
To confront
The smile beyond suffering,
As intricate and suffused
As a wave's curve
Just before it breaks.

Evanescence held still;
Change stated in eternal terms.
Aloof. Absolute:
The criterion is before us.

On my fiftieth birthday
I suffered from the archaic smile.

Mediterranean

Here is the ample place,
Hid in the sacred wood,
Where the intense young face
Meets the calm antique god,

Light flowing through the vine
Where air and earth are one;
Here are the sovereign wine,
The dark bread, the gold sun.

Distill all that's concrete
And make of it a prayer:
Air is the fig you eat;
The wine you drink is air.

This is the calm god's will,
And what he knows you know.
Lie under the terraced wall
And let the anguish go.

Let fall the torturing dream
Where the slow oxen move.
All things are what they seem
Here in the sacred grove.

Narcissus

His eyes are darker than he knows.
They flash out from a fire so deep
It draws him down to burning shadows.
It draws him further down than sleep.
And there in any quiet room
He faces a peculiar doom.
Within the mirror's empty face
His own eyes dreadfully expose
His solitary self, that place
He cannot leave, he cannot reach.
Whatever mirrors have to teach
He will learn now before he moves,
Lost in himself, but far from love.

It is not love that makes him fall
Deep into perilous reflection,
Not love that holds him there at all,
But rather something glimpsed and gone,
Angels and unicorns he sees
Vanish among the little trees,
Their lives so innocent and wise
That draw him into his own eyes,
Those fleeting selves that come quite near
But never tell him who they are.
He knows that he can never leave
Without the gift they have to give,
Powers that he must catch and tame
Or, drawn into the mirror, drown.

The Return of Aphrodite

Under the wave it is altogether still,
Alive and still, as nourishing as sleep,
Down below conflict, beyond need or will,
Where love flows on and yet is there to keep,
As unconstrained as waves that lift and break
And their bright foam neither to give nor take.

Listen to the long rising curve and stress,
Murmur of ocean that brings us the goddess.

From deep she rises, poised upon her shell.
Oh guiltless Aphrodite so long absent!
The green waves part. There is no sound at all
As she advances, tranquil and transparent,
To lay on mortal flesh her sacred mantle.

The wave recedes—she is drawn back again
Into the ocean where light leaves a stain.

Proteus

They were intense people, given to migraine,
Outbursts of arrogance, self-pity, or wild joy,
Affected by the weather like a weather vane,
Hungry for glory, exhausted by each day,
Humble at night and filled with self-distrust.
Time burned their heels. They ran because they must—

Sparkled, spilled over in the stress of living.
Oh, they were fickle, fluid, sometimes cruel,
Who still imagined they were always giving;
And the mind burned experience like fuel,
So they were sovereign losers, clumsy winners,
And read the saints, and knew themselves as sinners.

Wild blood subdued, it was pure form they blest.
Their sunlit landscapes were painted across pain.
They dreamed of peaceful gardens and of rest—
And now their joys, their joys alone remain.
Transparent, smiling, like calm gods to us,
Their names are Mozart, Rilke—Proteus.

Binding the Dragon

"The dragon's Proteus. He must be fought,
And fighting dragons is my holy joy,"
The poet says, although he may look caught
And blood is spurting from one eye.

"Sublimate," says the cautious analyst.
The poet answers, "Let him do it first.
Look, I have got this dragon in my fist.
I'll hold him here until he dies of thirst."

But suddenly the dragon flows away.
The dragon is a river: you can't do it,
Hold up a river in your hands all day.
"And what is sublimation?" asks the poet.

"Is it to translate water into fire?
Is it to follow birds along the air?
Is it to be the master of desire,
Or ride a cycle with no handlebar?

Gentle a dragon to lie quiet there,
Beautiful in his power but asleep,
Image of dragon resting on the air?"
The poet asked, and then began to weep.

He did not want the dragon to be caught.
He wanted it alive and in his fist.
For who would kill the god with whom he fought?
And so he wept and cursed the analyst.

The Phoenix

It is time the big bird with the angry neck,
We have cajoled and cursed,
Went home to die, or whatever he must do
When his heart would burst.

For his wild desire pulses over our heads
And opens the secret night,
Passage of wings that madden without release,
When the phoenix is in flight.

Let him go, stretching his long legs, clumsy
On this harsh ground. Let him flee
To the soft black marshes he remembers
Or the gentle mother tree.

Let him go. He has shaken the house at night;
His wings have clouded our dream,
And there is no peace for his lost cry at daybreak
And at night his terrible scream.

He flames through the morning yet he never sings;
He only makes that strange lost cry.
He is angry all the time. Let him find his tree
And make his nest and die.

Though he is God's own angel in disguise,
We cannot bear another angry word,
Nor look into those cold and jeweled eyes,
O pitiless strange bird!

Will he come back, will he come back all shining
From his dark death, to bring
The true message, the gentle, that all his torment
Was desperate to sing?

Or—what if it were not he at all, not he
Who must consume himself to be reborn,
But we ourselves, who drove an angel from us
Because our hearts were torn?

The Furies

One is large and lazy;
One is old and crazy;
One is young and witty;
One is a great beauty,
But all feed you the wind,
And each of them is blind.

How then to recognize
The hard unseeing eyes,
Or woman tell from ghost?
Human each is, almost—
That wild and glittering light—
Almost, and yet not quite.

Never look straight at one,
For then your self is gone.
The empty eyes give back
Your own most bitter lack,
And what they have to tell
Is your most secret Hell:

The old, the sad pursuit
Of the corrupting fruit,
The slightly tainted dish
Of the subconscious wish,
Fame, love, or merely pride
Exacerbate, provide.

Wrap you in glamor cold,
Warm you with fairy gold,
Till you grow fond and lazy,
Witty, perverse, and crazy,
And drink their health in wind,
And call the Furies kind.

Myth

The temple stood, holy and perfect,
Each pillar bearing its limit of strain serenely,
Balance and order shining in the dark.

And then a rush of swans' wings in the air,
A shower of stars. Thunder. All cracked apart.
Disorder of marble. Pockets of violet shadow.
Strange black gashes filled with the thrust of flowers.
The single arch which had enclosed the heart
Split open to the huge arches of the dark.

There was a rush of swans' wings through the air.

And those who had built the temple with such care
Came to a splendor of ruins,
Saw the perspectives altered
And all the pillars thrown to the ground,
And silent in their astonishment,
Learned what the gods can do.

Memory of Swans

The memory of swans comes back to you in sleep;
The landscape is a currentless still stream
Where reeds and rushes stand fast-rooted, deep.
And there the marvelous swan, more white than cream,
More warm than snow, moves as if silence loved him,
Where the dark supple waters ripple and enlace
The soft curve of the breast but have not moved him,
Where fluid passion yields to that cold grace.

So swans proceed, a miracle of pomp across your sleep,
The birds of silence, perfect form and balanced motion:
How will you fashion love, how will you wake and keep
The pride, the purity of a great image freed of its emotion?

Nostalgia for India

In the clean, anodyne
Hotel room in Athens,
I am suddenly homesick for
The Indian night
And my dark cell
In Orissa
Where I was visited
By a white lizard
With emerald eyes,
By an articulate frog,
And sometimes, very late,
By a wandering shrew.
The lizard chittered
And danced;
The shrew ran compulsively
Along the wall;
The frog,
When I lifted him up,
Gave a single heart-rending cry.
In my unmysterious
White room,
I miss the chittering,
The cry of despair,
The silent, lunatic trot—
It is too sane here for words.

The Godhead as Lynx

Kyrie Eleison, O wild lynx!
Mysterious sad eyes, and yet so bright,
Wherein mind never grieves or thinks,
But absolute attention is alight—
Before that golden gaze, so deep and cold,
My human rage dissolves, my pride is broken.
I am a child here in a world grown old.
Eons ago its final word was spoken.
Eyes of the god, hard as obsidian,
Look into mine. Kyrie Eleison.

Terrible as it is, your gaze consoles,
And awe turns tender before your guiltless head.
(What we have lost to enter into souls!)
I feel a longing for the lynx's bed,
To submerge self in that essential fur,
And sleep close to this ancient world of grace,
As if there could be healing next to her,
The mother-lynx in her prehuman place.
Yet that pure beauty does not know compassion—
O cruel god, Kyrie Eleison!

It is the marvelous world, free of our love,
Free of our hate, before our own creation,
Animal world, so still and so alive.
We never can go back to pure sensation,
Be self-possessed as the great lynx, or calm.
Yet she is lightning to cut down the lamb,
A beauty that devours without a qualm,
A cruel god who only says, "I am,"
Never, "You must become," as you, our own
God, say forever. Kyrie Eleison!

How rarely You look out from human eyes,
Yet it is we who bear creation on,
Troubled, afflicted, and so rarely wise,
Feeling nostalgia for an old world gone.
Imperfect as we are, and never whole,
Still You live in us like a fertile seed,

Always becoming, and asking of the soul
To stretch beyond sweet nature, answer need,
And lay aside the beauty of the lynx
To be this laboring self who groans and thinks.

Giant in the Garden

Innocence is the children's country, these
Full of wild pointless laughter, Christmas trees,
Birthdays gigantic when the self looms
Certain of greatness in the safer rooms,
Receives presents as its natural loot.
Innocence is not pure so much as pleased,
Always expectant, bright-eyed, self-enclosed,
But bursts into tears at a harsh word.
That self is lost when someone crashes through
To break the intact round I with a you.

The old really should not feel at home
In this fine country, safe as the womb.
The face without compassion, without guilt
Seems monstrous as the blank face of the pig
And children blush to discover the old baby
In grown-up language babbling secrets away.
It's even dangerous to play on alone
When all the children of your age have gone.
A willful giant looming in the garden
May like a mad dog one day go berserk
(Have you not heard the lewd and murderous bark?).

The Frog, that Naked Creature

The frog, that naked creature,
Arouses immediate pity;
He does not burst except in fables, but
He looks as if he might,
So violent his anxiety,
So exposed his nature.
His brilliant eyes look wildly out
As if the pulse were leaping from his throat.

We feel his being more, now
We have grown so vulnerable,
Have become so wholly exposed with the years
To primeval powers;
These storms are often terrible,
Followed by sudden snow.
It is alarming to feel the soul
Leap to the surface and find no sheltering wall.

Is this growth, we wonder?
But it makes us tremble,
Because we are not able to conceal
The rage, the fear we feel,
Nor able to dissemble
Those claps of thunder
When we are seized and shaken beyond our will
By the secret demon or the secret angel.

To show the very pulse
Of thought alive,
Transparent as the frog whose every mood
Glows through his cold red blood—
For whom we grieve
Because he has no walls—
Giving up pride, to endure shame and pity,
Is this a valid choice, choice of maturity?

A Village Tale

Why did the woman want to kill one dog?
Perhaps he was too lively, made her nervous,
A vivid terrier, restless, always barking,
And so unlike the gentle German shepherd.
She did not know herself what demon seized her,
How in the livid afternoon she was possessed,
What strength she found to tie a heavy stone
Around his neck and drown him in the horse-trough,
Murder her dog. God knows what drove her to it,
What strength she found to dig a shallow grave
And bury him—her own dog!—in the garden.

And all this while the gentle shepherd watched,
Said nothing, anxious nose laid on his paws,
Tail wagging dismal questions, watched her go
Into the livid afternoon outside to tire
The demon in her blood with wine and gossip.
The gate clanged shut, and the good shepherd ran,
Ran like a hunter to the quarry, hackles raised,
Sniffed the loose earth on the haphazard grave,
Pressing his eager nose into the dust,
Sensed tremor there and (frantic now) dug fast,
Dug in, dug in, all shivering and whining,
Unearthed his buried friend, licked the dry nose
Until a saving sneeze raised up the dead.

Well, she had to come back sometime to face
Whatever lay there waiting, worse than horror:
Two wagging tails, four bright eyes shifting—
Moment of truth, and there was no escape.
She could face murder. Could she face redeeming?

Was she relieved? Could she perhaps pretend
It had not really happened after all?
All that the village sees is that the dog
Sits apart now, untouchable and sacred,
Lazarus among dogs, whose loving eyes
Follow her back and forth until she dies.

She gives him tidbits. She can always try
To make them both forget the murderous truth.

But he knows and she knows that they are bound
Together in guilt and mercy, world without end.

The Fear of Angels

It is not what they intend,
But we are light-struck,
Blinded by their presence,
When all they want is to *see* us.

We have to turn away,
Cannot look at the huge, deep Unknown
That speaks through their eyes.
They strip us down to the infant gaze
Still deep in the sky,
Still rooted somewhere we cannot remember.

Angel, look away.
I cannot afford to yield the last defense,
To go back—

"Not back, but deeper,"
Said the angel, folding his wings
To wait.

The Lion and the Rose

Vision is locked in stone.
The lion in the air is gone
With the great lion of the sun.
The sky is wild and cold.
The tawny fire is gone.
The hill where love did open like a rose
Is black. It snows.

Emptiness flows.
The flowers in the heart all close
Drowned in a heavy white. Love knows
That poverty untold,
The cave where nothing grows.
The flaming lions of the flesh are gone,
Their power withdrawn.

God of the empty room,
Thy will be done. Thy will be done:
Now shine the inward sun,
The beating heart that glows
Within the skeleton,
The magic rose, the purer living gold,
Shine now, grown old.

All that is young and bold,
The lion's roar, the flaming skin and wild,
Unearthly peace now cherish and enfold
And fresh sleep overcome,
That in this death-in-life, delicate, cold,
The spiritual rose
Flower among the snows—

The love surpassing love.

Prayer before Work

Great one, austere,
By whose intent the distant star
Holds its course clear,
Now make this spirit soar—
Give it that ease.

Out of the absolute
Abstracted grief, comfortless, mute,
Sound the clear note,
Pure, piercing as the flute:
Give it precision.

Austere, great one,
By whose grace the inalterable song
May still be wrested from
The corrupt lung:
Give it strict form.

Prisoner at a Desk

It is not so much trying to keep alive
As trying to keep from blowing apart
From inner explosions every day.
I sit here, open to psychic changes,
Living myself as if I were a land,
Or mountain weather, the quick cycles
Where we are tossed from the ice age
To bursts of spring, to sudden torrents
Of rain like tears breaking through iron.
It is all I can do to keep tethered down.

No prisoner at a desk, but an ocean
Or forest where waves and gentle leaves
And strange wild beasts under the groves
And whales in all their beauty under the blue
Can gently rove together, still untamed,
Where all opens and breathes and can grow.

Whatever I have learned of good behavior
Withers before these primal powers.
Here at the center governess or censor
No longer has command. The soul is here,
Inviolable splendor that exists alone.

Prisoner at a desk? No, universe of feeling
Where everything is seen, and nothing mine
To plead with or possess, only partake of,
As if at times I could put out a hand
And touch the lion head, the unicorn.
Here there is nothing, no one, not a sound
Except the distant rumor, the huge cloud
Of archetypal images that feed me . . .

Look, there are finches at the feeder.
My parrot screams with fear at a cloud.
Hyacinths are budding. Light is longer.

A Letter to James Stephens

James, it is snowing here. It is November.
Think of the good day when we talked together,
For it is time to think of it, remember
What the warm wine, warm friendship, summer weather
Raised in our minds now that it is so cold,
Now that we sit alone and half the world apart,
This bitter season when the young grow old
And sit indoors to weigh the fiery heart:
What of it now? What of this personal all,
The little world these hands have tried to fashion
Using a single theme for their material,
Always a human heart, a human passion?
You said "Seek for a sterner stuff than this,
Look out of your closed spaces to the infinite,
Look beyond hunger and the longed-for kiss
To what there is beyond your love and in it,
To the whole heavy earth and all it bears;
Support the sky. Know the path of the planet,
Until you stand alone, a man who stares
His loneliness out of its depth to span it,
Till you can chisel substance out of space.
Forget your love, your little war, your ache;
Forget that haunting so mysterious face
And write for an abstracted beauty's sake.
Contain a large world in a small strict plan,
Your job is to draw out the essence and provide
The word that will endure, comfort, sustain a man.
This is your honor. This should be your pride."
Dear James, pure poet, I see you with that shell
Held to your sensitive abstracted ear,
Hunting the ocean's rumor till you hear it well,
Until you can set down the sound you hear:—
Fixed to a shell like that you made immortal,
This heart listens, this fragile auricle
Holds rumor like your ocean's, is a portal
That sometimes opens to contain the miracle.
If there are miracles we can record
They happen in the places that you curse.

Blessèd the pure in heart and the enduring word
Sings of that love that spins the universe.
My honor (and I cherish it for it is hardly won)
Is to be pure in this: is to believe
That to write down these perishable songs for one,
For one alone, and out of love, is not to grieve
But to build on the quicksand of despair
A house where every man may take his ease,
May come to shelter from the outer air,
A little house where he may find his peace.
Dear James, if this fire seems only the strange
Quick-burning fire of youth unfounded on the earth
Then may it be transformed but never change.
Let Him in whose hands lie death and birth
Preserve its essence like that bush of flame
That stood up in a path, and, fiery-plumed,
Contained the angel who could speak God's name—
The bush that burned and still was not consumed.

The Work of Happiness

I thought of happiness, how it is woven
Out of the silence in the empty house each day
And how it is not sudden and it is not given
But is creation itself like the growth of a tree.
No one has seen it happen, but inside the bark
Another circle is growing in the expanding ring.
No one has heard the root go deeper in the dark,
But the tree is lifted by this inward work
And its plumes shine, and its leaves are glittering.

So happiness is woven out of the peace of hours
And strikes its roots deep in the house alone:
The old chest in the corner, cool waxed floors,
White curtains softly and continually blown
As the free air moves quietly about the room;
A shelf of books, a table, and the white-washed wall—
These are the dear familiar gods of home,
And here the work of faith can best be done,
The growing tree is green and musical.

For what is happiness but growth in peace,
The timeless sense of time when furniture
Has stood a life's span in a single place,
And as the air moves, so the old dreams stir
The shining leaves of present happiness?
No one has heard thought or listened to a mind,
But where people have lived in inwardness
The air is charged with blessing and does bless;
Windows look out on mountains and the walls are kind.

An Intruder

The other day a witch came to call.
She brought a basket full of woe and gall
And left it there for me in my front hall.

But it was empty when I found it there
And she herself had gone back to her lair
Leaving the bats of rage to fly my air.

Out of ambivalence this witch was born;
All that she gives is subtly smeared and torn
Or slightly withered by her love and scorn.

The furies sit and watch me as I write;
The bats fly silently about all night
And a black mist obscures the kindest light.

But I shall find the magic note to play,
Or, like a donkey, learn the wild flat bray
That sends all furies howling on their way.

The note is laughter. No witch could withstand
The frightful joke all witches understand
When they are given all that they demand.

The word can neither bless nor curse, of course.
It must bewitch a witch and leave her worse.
Perhaps I'll call her just a failed old nurse.

Love cannot exorcize the gifts of hate.
Hate cannot exorcize what has no weight,
But laughter we can never over-rate.

Now I Become Myself

Now I become myself. It's taken
Time, many years and places;
I have been dissolved and shaken,
Worn other people's faces,
Run madly, as if Time were there,
Terribly old, crying a warning,
"Hurry, you will be dead before—"
(What? Before you reach the morning?
Or the end of the poem is clear?
Or love safe in the walled city?)
Now to stand still, to be here,
Feel my own weight and density!
The black shadow on the paper
Is my hand; the shadow of a word
As thought shapes the shaper
Falls heavy on the page, is heard.
All fuses now, falls into place
From wish to action, word to silence,
My work, my love, my time, my face
Gathered into one intense
Gesture of growing like a plant.
As slowly as the ripening fruit
Fertile, detached, and always spent,
Falls but does not exhaust the root,
So all the poem is, can give,
Grows in me to become the song;
Made so and rooted so by love.
Now there is time and Time is young.
O, in this single hour I live
All of myself and do not move.
I, the pursued, who madly ran,
Stand still, stand still, and stop the sun!

My Sisters, O My Sisters

Nous qui voulions poser, image ineffaceable
Comme un delta divin notre main sur le sable
Anna de Noailles

I

Dorothy Wordsworth, dying, did not want to read,
"I am too busy with my own feelings," she said.

And all women who have wanted to break out
Of the prison of consciousness to sing or shout

Are strange monsters who renounce the treasure
Of their silence for a curious devouring pleasure.

Dickinson, Rossetti, Sappho—they all know it,
Something is lost, strained, unforgiven in the poet.

She abdicates from life or like George Sand
Suffers from the mortality in an immortal hand,

Loves too much, spends a whole life to discover
She was born a good grandmother, not a good lover.

Too powerful for men: Madame de Stael. Too sensitive:
Madame de Sévigné, who burdened where she meant to give.

Delicate as that burden was and so supremely lovely,
It was too heavy for her daughter, much too heavy.

Only when she built inward in a fearful isolation
Did any one succeed or learn to fuse emotion

With thought. Only when she renounced did Emily
Begin in the fierce lonely light to learn to be.

Only in the extremity of spirit and the flesh
And in renouncing passion did Sappho come to bless.

Only in the farewells or in old age does sanity
Shine through the crimson stains of their mortality.

And now we who are writing women and strange monsters
Still search our hearts to find the difficult answers,

Still hope that we may learn to lay our hands
More gently and more subtly on the burning sands.

To be through what we make more simply human,
To come to the deep place where poet becomes woman,

Where nothing has to be renounced or given over
In the pure light that shines out from the lover,

In the warm light that brings forth fruit and flower
And that great sanity, that sun, the feminine power.

VII

The Action of Therapy

This is no repetition
Of unresolved attachments
And deprivations,
No turn of the old wheel.
It is altogether new.

The Action of Therapy

1

After the whirlwind when all things
Were blown out of their courses
In the fiery gust,
After the whirlwind when all beams were crossed
And passionate love confused,
Its clear path lost,
Where nothing fused,
But all was burned and forced,
The psyche nearly cracked
Under the blast,
After the earthquake passed

How did it happen
That cool eyes looked out
On darkness and the storm
And cut the ties
That meant chaos and harm
So that true mysteries
Might act and charm
The haunted spirit back
To its own realm?

What did the angel do
To make all levels straight
Within that sheaf
Of troubled sense and fear,
Set every beam on its own path
At last untangled,
Singular and bright,
So that nothing was lost,
No slightest hope
Was blurred by childish grief
Outside its scope,
But all was still and clear,
So still and bright
No galaxy of stars

Could shine more absolute
On winter night?

2

I watched the psychic surgeon,
Stern, skilled, adroit,
Cut deep into the heart
And yet not hurt.
I watched it happen—
Old failures, old obsessions
Cut away
So blood could flow
A clear course through
Choked arteries again.
There was no pain.
My eyes, wide open,
Watched every move
In absolute surrender
To superior power.
I saw it happen
In one luminous hour
(No anesthetic given),
An act of extreme grace
And sovereign love.
From Hell I entered Heaven
And bowed my head,
Where nothing had been suffered,
But all given.

3

Simple acceptance
Of things as they are;
Finished, that strained arc,
Leap of the salmon upstream
Climbing waterfalls,
Sublimation
Of one death or another,

The cruel ascension
Toward loss.

Now things as they are—
Spring of the fern as it uncoils,
Brute rock broken
To show the crystal,
Light-shot February skies—
All, all have been given
After the whirlwind.

This is no repetition
Of unresolved attachments
And deprivations,
No turn of the old wheel.
It is altogether new.

4

In the terrifying whirlwind
When the mother is resurrected
(How many times, angelic doctor,
How many times?)
Every defense against grief goes.
There is no future,
Only excruciating repetition
Of the unburied past.
For the last time
I was torn to pieces
By my mother's anguish,
Unattainable goddess
Whose compassionate eyes
Understood me so well—
And took my heart.

I do not have to love you
As I loved her,
To be devastated, but,
Angel and surgeon of the psyche,
I am free to love you now

Outside all the myths,
The confused dreams,
Beyond all the barriers,
In the warm natural light
Of simple day.
I am allowed to give you
Unstrained, flowing,
Wise-infant
To wise-mother love.

You broke the spell;
You with your whippets around you
Like some lady in a tapestry
Said to the unicorn,
"If the child needs the mother,
The mother needs the child."
So be it.

5

In middle age we starve
For ascension,
Look back to childhood teachers
But have outgrown them.
Mature love needs new channels.
How long has it been—
What starving years—
Since I was permitted
To cherish wisdom?
I bend tenderly
Toward the young
With open heart and hands.
I share in a great love
With my equal.
Every day I learn better
About how to give
And how to receive love.
But there is still the need
To be filial toward someone,

To be devoted,
Humble and enlightened.
I need to remain teachable
For one who can teach me.
With you all green things flourish,
All flowers may be freely given,
All fears can be expressed,
No childish need is sneered at,
No adult gift unrecognized.

Speak to me
Of the communion of saints
On earth.

6

Light cannot be described,
Is nothing in itself,
Transforms all it touches.
The flower becomes transparent flame.
A plain white wall
Is marbled by flowing water,
And in the soul's realm
Light defines feeling,
Makes distinctions.

In the light
Of this penetrating mind,
Vivid response,
Total awareness,
I find myself
In a new landscape—
Fra Angelico's Paradise
(It was dear to my mother
I suddenly remember)
Where souls, released at last,
Dance together
On the simple grass.

Look, there is an owl in the tree;
A fling of lambs in February snow.
There is a donkey waving her long ears.
There is a child
With flowers in her hands.

There is a continuum
(Those garlands of joined dancers)
Of redemptive love.

I'll keep it
For a million years.

Index